ESSENTIAL ANTHOLOGY

CREATIVITY AND IMAGINATION

Jane Branson

Ken Haworth

Beth Kemp

Trevor Millum

OXFORD

UNIVERSITY PRESS

Great Clarendon Street, Oxford, OX2 6DP, United Kingdom

Oxford University Press is a department of the University of Oxford.
It furthers the University's objective of excellence in research, scholarship,
and education by publishing worldwide. Oxford is a registered trade mark of
Oxford University Press in the UK and in certain other countries

British Library Cataloguing in Publication Data
Data available

978-1-4085-2340-7

1 3 5 7 9 10 8 6 4 2

Page make-up by EMC Design

Printed and bound in Spain

Image acknowledgements

Illustrations

pp 3, **4**, **7**, **32**, **44–45**, **80** Bridget Dowty
pp 14–15, **21**, **37**, **40–41**, **60–61**, **92** Élisabeth Eudes-Pascal
pp 8–9, **18–19**, **42–43**, **55**, **56–57**, **71**, **83** Sarah Kirk
pp 33, **49**, **58**, **69**, **70**, **73**, **74** Paul McCaffrey
pp 10, **27**, **34**, **52**, **63**, **64–65**, **91** Bob Moulder

Photographs

The publishers would like to thank the following for permission to use their
photographs:

p2: Africa Studio/Fotolia; **pp11–13**: AnikaSalsera/iStockphoto; **pp16–17**:
Gordan/Shutterstock; **p20**: Lobke Peers/Shutterstock; **p22**: Kuvaario/
Alamy; **p23**: Javarman/Alamy; **p24**: Coast-to-Coast/iStockphoto; **p25**:
hphimagelibrary/iStockphoto; **p26**: Paul Adams – North West Images/
Alamy; **p28**: CarlaMc/iStockphoto; **p29**: mauritius images GmbH/Alamy;
p30: Simon Belcher/Alamy; **p31**: Naomi Calverd; **p35**: godrick/iStockphoto;
p36: Fadtukhin/iStockphoto; **p38**: steps/iStockphoto; **p39**: Gizmo/
iStockphoto; **pp46–47**: Fer Gregory/Shutterstock; **p50**: AF archive/Alamy;
p54: imagedepotpro/iStockphoto; **p59**: tigermad/iStockphoto; **pp66–67**:
Cora Mueller/Shutterstock; **p68**: v.s.anandhakrishna/Shutterstock; **p75**:
okeyphotos/iStockphoto; **p76**: SoulOfAutumn/iStockphoto; **p77**: eric1513/
iStockphoto; **p78**: heckmannoleg/iStockphoto; **p79**: Gucio_55/Fotolia; **p81**:
Mar Photographics/Alamy; D. Hurst/Alamy; **p82**: Llepod/iStockphoto; Triff/
Shutterstock; **pp84–85**: wragg/iStockphoto; **pp86–87**: dan_prat/iStockphoto;
p88: ABACA/ABACA/Press Association Images; **p89**: MIKE HUTCHINGS/
Reuters/Corbis; **pp89–90**: UIG via Getty Images.

Contents

Contents

Introduction by Imelda Pilgrim

Reading is at the heart of many things we do in our lives; without the ability to read we would not be able to understand messages, posters, surveys, leaflets, bank statements and application forms. But there is much more to it than this. Reading can open up new worlds to us and make us look again at the world in which we live. It can inform our knowledge of historical and current events, prompt us to reflect on our own lives and relationships, raise our awareness of other cultures and other ways of thinking, and allow us to enter imagined worlds created in the minds of others.

This anthology is packed with material from a wide range of sources for you to read, but it is not just your reading skills that will improve from studying them. The texts have also been selected with the aim of having a direct impact on both your writing and your spoken English skills. Studying well-constructed pieces of writing can help you to become more competent in developing and organising ideas, and in expressing these in Standard English. In addition, they provide a model for the effective use of vocabulary and phrasing, and for accuracy in the essential skills of spelling and punctuation.

The book is divided into five units.

Unit 1: Stepping into stories contains a range of texts from various periods of literature. There are excerpts from novels, short stories and a fictional diary, all of which you can use to develop your skills in identifying and analysing purpose, audience and context.

Unit 2: The many possibilities of poetry provides a range of poems that will not only enable you to develop your skills in close and careful reading, but might also encourage you to try to write poetry yourself.

Unit 3: From page to stage is made up of a variety of script extracts, from Shakespeare to the modern day. These will help you to learn about the particular skills involved in writing for the stage, as distinct from novels, short stories and poetry.

Unit 4: Writing creatively features a range of fiction and non-fiction sources, some of which are linked by themes, including violence, love and loss. This collection of texts will enable you to explore the techniques involved in writing creatively, which in turn will help you in your own writing.

Unit 5: Exploration comprises a range of genres linked by theme. It revisits the main areas of study in Units 1 to 4 and provides an opportunity for you to use and consolidate your learning.

As you study each text, your teacher will lead you through a range of activities designed to develop your understanding and your skills in reading, writing, and spoken English. Aim to pay close attention to detail, learn from the craft of the writers and the designers, consider the potential effects of the spoken word, and, most importantly, share your ideas and ask probing questions.

Introduction

In this unit, you will read texts by authors with a range of approaches and styles from various periods of literature. The texts appear in the order you might read them, but you can also look at them in pairs and groups, noticing similarities and differences between them.

There are extracts from two older novels in this unit – *Gulliver's Travels* and *Oliver Twist* – as well as from two modern novels *Abomination* and *Noah Barleywater Runs Away.* The contemporary extracts have a similar main theme – they are both about a child in trouble. The narrative style of the two authors, however, is very different.

There are two short stories in this unit: 'Significant Moments in the Life of My Mother' and 'The Guitarist'. One is an extract from a tale with autobiographical elements; the other is a complete ghost story.

The Secret Diary of Adrian Mole aged 13¾ is different again. It is written in the style of a teenage boy's diary, and mainly aims to entertain. But it has a satirical edge, poking fun at its own main character.

During this unit, you will develop a variety of skills and these will add to your enjoyment of reading. For example, you'll be comparing genres and fictional features, and using clues in the texts. You'll be exploring the purpose, audience and context of each piece of writing.

You will also be developing your own writing skills. You'll be asked to produce essays for different purposes, a formal speech and narratives in different styles. As you complete the reading and writing tasks, you will be taking part in speaking activities too.

TEXT 1

In *Abomination* by Robert Swindells, Martha tells of life with her parents, members of a strict religious group. In Chapter 3, Martha describes her typical evening, and hints at family secrets. By Chapter 58, Martha's parents have discovered she has a forbidden friend and have decided to move house to keep their secrets safe.

- What has happened to Martha in the time between these two chapters?
- What is the effect of the first-person narrative in these extracts?
- What do you think about Martha's life?

ABOMINATION
CHAPTER 3: **MARTHA**

My favourite time is dinner time when I have the place to myself. Father's an agent for an insurance company. He does his round at night because that's when people are in, and Mother works the evening shift at a soft toy factory.

I have the washing-up to do and Abomination's[1] mess to see to, but after that I'm free till ten, except in winter when it's nine thirty. We don't have TV. I sometimes listen to Radio One, but I've got to remember not to leave the set tuned to that station when I switch off, because the Righteous believe that the devil reaches young people through pop music. The Righteous is our church. One night last year I forgot, and when Father switched on for the morning news he got Madonna and I got the rod. It's a cane really, but Father calls it the rod. His favourite text is *Train up a child in the way he should go: and when he is old, he will not depart from it.* Notice it

[1] a thing that causes disgust or hatred – here it refers to a child

says he, not she. It's not about girls, but Father seems not to have spotted that and I daren't point it out.

They're administered really carefully by the way, my beatings. Oh, yes. Wouldn't do for some busybody to spot the marks on me. They're always on my bum, so they're covered in PE and even when I swim. I could show somebody of course, but then Father would get into trouble and I wouldn't want to be responsible for that. He thinks he's doing the best thing, you see: that it's for my own good.

Anyway, after twirling round the kitchen to a few of the devil's tunes, I usually go up to my room and look at Mary's postcards. Mary's my big sister. Father sent her away when I was six. She's grown up and has a really interesting life if the cards are anything to go by. They're from all over: London, Liverpool, Birmingham. There's even one from Amsterdam. Some are addressed to Mother and Father and some are to me. I'm not supposed to have any of them. Father tears them up unread and throws them in the bin, but I rescue them and stick them back together with sellotape. I've been doing this since I was six. I couldn't read then, but I knew who they were from and the pictures were nice. I've got thirty-one now, in a shoe-box under the floor, with my Blur poster, four *Point Horror*[2] books and a few other things my parents wouldn't like.

Mother says we're special because we're Righteous, but that doesn't make me feel any better. I'd rather not be special if it means having to hide things.

If I can't have friends around.

If I can't have friends.

CHAPTER 58: MARTHA

I had a rotten night. Well, rotten in one way, thrilling in another. I got into bed without undressing because I expected Mary any minute, but the longer I lay there the more doubtful I felt about those calls. I mean, I'd no *proof* it was Scott. Father might be right – it could have

been some sci-fi freak on alcopop. As time crawled by and nothing happened, this seemed more and more likely. And if it wasn't Scott – if Scott hadn't even been near – my notice would be on next door's fence in the morning for all to see. For Father to see.

I prayed. Not my usual bedtime prayer. This was the prayer of a screwed-up kid who's had just about enough. *Dear God, I know Mother and Father will have spoken to you about this, but it surely can't be right to keep a child in a cage. Maybe you told them and they misheard. I don't want to get them in trouble and I don't mean to be wicked. I just think a kid's entitled to some love and sunshine, and how did that get into my head if you didn't put it there? Please let Mary come soon. Amen.*

I think I slept after that, because the next thing I knew it was light and I could hear a blackbird. I got up and straightened my clothes a bit, though my stuff always looks slept in anyway. I washed my hands and face, brushed my hair and went downstairs. My parents were at table. We said good morning. Mother served the porridge. The kid was kicking up a fuss below. It was just like any other Saturday morning. I wondered whether Scott would try Asda as usual.

'Mother?'

'What is it, Martha?'

'Do you need anything from the supermarket this morning?'

'I don't think so, thank you. We can make do till we move, and shop in Wharton on Tuesday evening.'

'Oh.' My heart sank. I'd hoped to remove my notice *and* see Scott.

'There's something you *can* do,' said Father. 'When you've attended to Abomination, you can take a screwdriver to your room and free your furniture from the walls, ready for the removal men.'

---

[2] a series of horror books published for teenagers and young adults

'Yes, Father.' If prayers are answered, Mary'd have come and none of this dreary stuff would be happening. *Prayers aren't answered*, I thought, as I trailed down those cellar steps for the two thousandth time. I was nearly crying.

A few minutes later I was wiping slop from round the kid's mouth when someone knocked on the front door. *Postman*, I told myself, guarding against the cruelty of false hope. I dropped the cloth in the basin and reached for the pack of disposable nappies. I heard Father turn the key, draw the bolt. *Some boring package*, I thought. *Tracts. A double glazing catalogue.*

'YOU!' Father's voice, startled and outraged at the same time. *Who? Scott? No*. A woman's voice. *Not... surely not Mary?* I rose to my feet, staring towards the steps. The kid, cold in his sodden nappy, began to grizzle.

'I want my child,' shrilled the voice. 'Give him to me NOW!'

'Child?' spluttered Father. 'Have you gone MAD? The child isn't here. It was adopted, six years ago. We don't even know...'

'He's *there*, in that cellar. Martha e-mailed. Let me pass, or I'll ...'

'E-mail? *Martha* e-mail? Now I know you're mad. There's no e-mail here. Lizzy!' He called to Mother. 'Come here and tell this lunatic ... this strumpet, that her bast...'

And that's when something really weird happened inside my head. Really really weird. I think it was the words *my child* that did it. I looked at the kid and it was like I saw him for the very first time as a kid. He wasn't the monster I'd once believed him to be, and he wasn't the nuisance I'd been saddled with. He was neither a chore nor a shameful secret; he was a child: a frail, beautiful, grey-eyed child who should be out in the sunshine with other six-year-olds, not cooped up and mucked out

and fed through the bars like a battery hen. I gazed at him and knew at last the enormity of the wrong I'd helped commit.

I ran sobbing to the foot of the stairs. 'MARY!' My voice broke up. 'HE'S HERE.' Father growled an oath and there were sounds of a scuffle. Mother began to wail. I turned, scooped the kid out of the playpen and started up the steps. He was light. Almost weightless. Father was standing at the top with his back to me and his arms spread, blocking my progress and my sister's view but the end was in sight and nothing was going to stop me finishing it now. Nothing. I twisted sideways and rammed my shoulder into the small of his back. He didn't move much, but the woman got a glimpse of her child and that was enough. She flung Mother from her, side-stepped Father, snatched the kid out of my arms and half-ran towards the open door. The child covered his eyes with his hands and began to scream. It was the light streaming through the doorway. The sunlight. He'd never encountered such brightness. It seared him, and to find himself bouncing towards it in the arms of a total stranger must have been more terrifying than any of us can imagine. I was imagining what my parents would do to me after Mary had gone, when she paused and turned, her free hand held out towards me.

'Come on, Marfa, quick!'

The thought that I'd be rescued too hadn't entered my head but I didn't hesitate, following this thin, dowdy stranger out the door and down the path to where another stranger sat in the driving seat of an ancient car whose engine was idling. The last thing I saw as acceleration slammed me back in the seat was Mother on the doorstep looking like someone beholding the end of the world.

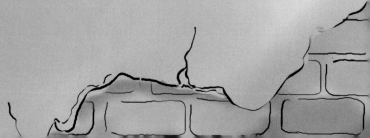

TEXT 2

In these opening paragraphs of John Boyne's novel, *Noah Barleywater Runs Away*, the author creates a first impression of the main character and sets up a mystery: why is this boy running away from home?

- How would you be feeling if you were leaving home for ever? How many achievements would be on your list?
- This novel is written in what we call third-person narrative. Would you react differently if the author had used the first person 'I'?

NOAH BARLEYWATER RUNS AWAY

Noah Barleywater left home in the early morning, before the sun rose, before the dogs woke, before the dew stopped falling on the fields.

He climbed out of bed and shuffled into the clothes he'd laid out the night before, holding his breath as he crept quietly downstairs. Three of the steps had a loud creak in them where the wood didn't knit together correctly so he walked very softly on each one, desperate to make as little noise as possible.

In the hallway he took his coat off the hook but didn't put his shoes on until he had already left the house. He walked down the laneway, opened the gate, went through and closed it again, treading as lightly as he could in case his parents heard the sound of the gravel crunching beneath his feet and came downstairs to investigate.

It was still dark at this hour and Noah had to squint to make out the road that twisted and turned up ahead. The growing light would allow him to sense any danger that might be lurking in the shadows. When he got to the end of the first quarter-mile, at just that point where he could turn round one last time and still make out his home in the distance, he stared at the smoke rising from the chimney that stretched upwards from the kitchen fireplace and thought of his family inside, all safely tucked up in their beds, unaware that he was leaving them for ever. And despite himself, he felt a little sad.

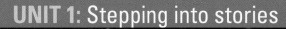

Am I doing the right thing? he wondered, a great blanket of happy memories trying to break through and smother the fresher, sadder ones.

But he had no choice. He couldn't bear to stay any longer. No one could blame him for that, surely. Anyway, it was probably best that he went out to make his own way in the world. After all, he was already eight years old and the truth was, he hadn't really done anything with his life so far.

A boy in his class, Charlie Charlton, had appeared in the local newspaper when he was only seven, because the Queen had come to open a day centre for all the grannies and grandads in the village, and he had been chosen to hand her a bunch of flowers and say, *We're SO delighted you could make the journey, ma'am.* A photograph had been taken where Charlie was grinning like the Cheshire cat[1] as he presented the bouquet, and the Queen wore an expression that suggested she had smelled something funny but was far too well-brought-up to comment on it; he'd seen that expression on the Queen's face before and it always make him giggle. The photo had been placed on the school notice board the following day and had remained there until someone – *not* Noah – had drawn a moustache on Her Majesty's face and written some rude words in a speech bubble coming out of her mouth that nearly gave the headmaster, Mr Tushingham, a stroke.

The whole thing had caused a terrible scandal, but at least Charlie Charlton had got his face in the papers and been the toast of the schoolyard for a few days. What had Noah ever done with his life to compare with that? Nothing. Why, only a few days before he'd tried to make a list of all his achievements, and this is what he'd come up with:

1. *I have read fourteen books from cover to cover.*
2. *I won the bronze medal in the 500 metres at Sports Day last year and would have won silver if Breiffni O'Neill hadn't jumped the gun and got a head start.*
3. *I know the capital of Portugal. (It's Lisbon.)*
4. *I may be small for my age but I'm the seventh cleverest boy in my class.*
5. *I am an excellent speller.*

Five achievements at eight years of age, he thought at the time, shaking his head and pressing the tip of his pencil to his tongue, even though his teacher, Miss Bright, screamed whenever anyone did that and said they would get lead poisoning. *That's one achievement for every ...* He thought about it and did a series of quick calculations on a bit of scrap paper. *One achievement for every one year, seven months and six days. Not very impressive at all.*

He tried to tell himself that this was the reason he was leaving home, because it seemed a lot more adventurous than the real reason, which was something he didn't want to think about. Not this early in the morning, anyway.

---

[1] a cat with a broad, fixed grin, who appears in the classic children's book *Alice in Wonderland*

Margaret Atwood is one of the most important writers of our times. She writes poetry, short stories, novels and essays. As she often draws on her childhood in the backwoods of Quebec in Canada, much of her work – like this story – seems to be autobiographical.

- What information does the narrator give us that shows how life has changed since the moment described?
- How are different tenses used in the story?
- What features of story-writing and autobiography do you notice in this text? What genre do you think fits it best?

SIGNIFICANT MOMENTS IN THE
LIFE OF MY MOTHER

There are photographs of my mother at this time,[1] taken with three or four other girls, linked arm in arm or with their arms thrown jestingly around each other's necks. Behind them, beyond the sea or the hills or whatever is in the background, is a world already hurtling towards ruin, unknown to them: the theory of relativity has been discovered, acid is accumulating at the roots of trees, the bull-frogs are doomed. But they smile with something that from this distance you could almost call gallantry, their right legs thrust forward in parody of a chorus line.[2]

One of the great amusements for the girl boarders[3] and the sons of the family was amateur theatre. Young people – they were called "young people" – frequently performed in plays which were put on in the church basement. My mother was a regular actor. (I have a stack of the scripts somewhere about the house, yellowing little booklets with my mother's parts checked in pencil. They are all comedies, and all impenetrable.) "There was no television then," says my mother. "You made your own fun."

For one of these plays a cat was required, and my mother and one of the sons borrowed the family cat. They put it into a canvas bag and drove to the rehearsal (there were cars by then), with my mother holding the cat on her lap. The cat, which must have been frightened, wet itself copiously, through the canvas bag and all over my mother's skirt. At the same time it made the most astonishingly bad smell.

"I was ready to sink through the floorboards," says my mother. "But what could I do? All I could do was sit there. In those days things like that" – she means cat pee, or pee of any sort – "were not mentioned." She means in mixed company.[4]

I think of my mother driven through the night, skirts dripping, overcome with shame, the young man beside her staring straight ahead, pretending not to notice anything. They both feel that this act of unmentionable urination has been done, not by the cat, but by my mother. And so they continue, in a straight line that takes them over the Atlantic and past the curvature of the earth, out through the moon's orbit and into the dark reaches beyond.

Meanwhile, back on earth, my mother says: "I had to throw the skirt out. It was a good skirt, too, but nothing could get rid of the smell."

---

[1] the 1920s – the narrator's mother was seventeen

[2] a line of dancers in a show

[3] young people lodging with a family

[4] men and women together

TEXT 4

Sue Townsend's *The Secret Diary of Adrian Mole aged 13¾* is a comic novel written as a diary. In this extract, early on, it is already obvious that we can't trust what Adrian says – notice how obsessed he is with a spot on his chin that no one else can even see!

- How does the diary style contribute to the effect on the reader?
- What can you tell about life in the 1980s from Adrian's diary?

The Secret Diary of ADRIAN MOLE aged 13¾

Sunday January 17th

I was woken up early this morning. Mrs Lucas is concreting the front of their house and the concrete lorry had to keep its engine running while she shovelled the concrete round before it set. Mr Lucas made her a cup of tea. He really is kind.

Nigel came round to see if I wanted to go to the pictures but I told him I couldn't, because I was going to the doctor's about the spot. He said he couldn't see a spot, but he was just being polite because the spot is massive today.

Dr Taylor must be one of those overworked GPs you are always reading about. He didn't examine the spot, he just said I mustn't worry and was everything all right at home. I told him about my bad home life and my poor diet, but he said I was well nourished and to go home and count my blessings. So much for the National Health Service.

I will get a paper-round and go private.

Sunday January 18th

SECOND AFTER EPIPHANY. OXFORD HILARY TERM STARTS

Mrs Lucas and my mother have had a row over the dog. Somehow it escaped from the house and trampled on Mrs Lucas's wet concrete. My father offered to have the dog put down, but my mother started to cry so he said he wouldn't. All the neighbours were out in the street washing their cars and listening. Sometimes I really hate that dog!

I remembered my resolution about helping the poor and ignorant today, so I took some of my old Beano annuals to a quite poor family who have moved into the next street. I know they are poor because they have only got a black and white telly. A boy answered the door. I explained why I had come. He looked at the annuals and said, 'I've read 'em', and slammed the door in my face. So much for helping the poor!

Monday January 19th

I have joined a group at school called the Good Samaritans. We go out into the community helping and stuff like that. We miss Maths on Monday afternoons.

Today we had a talk on the sort of things we will be doing. I have been put in the old age pensioners' group. Nigel has got a dead yukky job looking after kids in a playgroup. He is as sick as a parrot.

I can't wait for next Monday. I will get a cassette so I can tape all the old fogies' stories about the war and stuff. I hope I get one with a good memory.

The dog is back at the vet's. It has got concrete stuck on its paws. No wonder it was making such a row on the stairs last night. Pandora smiled at me in school dinner today, but I was choking on a piece of gristle so I couldn't smile back. Just my luck!

Tuesday January 20th

FULL MOON

My mother is looking for a job!

And what will I do during the holidays? I expect I will have to sit in a launderette all day to keep warm. I will be a latchkey kid,[1] whatever that is. And who will look after the dog? And what will I have to eat all day? I will be forced to eat crisps and sweets until my skin is ruined and my teeth fall out. I think my mother is being very selfish. She won't be any good in a job anyway. She isn't very bright and she drinks too much at Christmas.

I rang my grandma up and told her, and she says I could stay at her house in the holidays, and go to the Evergreens[12] meetings in the afternoons and stuff like that. I wish I hadn't rung now. The Samaritans met today during break. The old people were shared out. I got an old man called Bert Baxter. He is eighty-nine so I don't suppose I'll have him for long. I'm going round to see him tomorrow. I hope he hasn't got a dog. I'm fed up with dogs. They are either at the vet's or standing in front of the television.

Wednesday January 21st

Mr and Mrs Lucas are getting a divorce![3] They are the first down our road. My mother went next door to comfort Mr Lucas. He must have been very upset because she was still there when my father came home from work. Mrs Lucas has gone somewhere in a taxi. I think she has left for ever because she has taken her socket set with her. Poor Mr Lucas, now he will have to do his own washing and stuff.

My father cooked the tea tonight. We had boil-in-the-bag curry and rice, it was the only thing left in the freezer apart from a bag of green stuff which has lost its label. My father made a joke about sending it to the public health inspector. My mother didn't laugh. Perhaps she was thinking about poor Mr Lucas left on his own.

I went to see old Mr Baxter after tea. My father dropped me off on his way to play badminton. Mr Baxter's house is hard to see from the road. It has got a massive overgrown privet hedge all round it. When I knocked on the door a dog started barking and growling and jumping up at the letterbox. I heard the sound of bottles being knocked over and a man swearing before I ran off. I hope I got the wrong number.

I saw Nigel on the way home. He told me Pandora's father is a milkman! I have gone off her a bit.

Nobody was in when I got home so I fed the dog, looked at my spots and went to bed.

---

[1] a child who returns home on their own at the end of the day, so needs his/her own key

[2] a social group attended by Adrian's grandmother

[3] the number of divorces increased steadily up to the early 1980s, but has been declining since the mid-90s

TEXT 5

Charles Dickens' *Oliver Twist* was first published (1837–39) in a series of monthly instalments, keeping readers gripped with suspense as the story was gradually revealed. At this point in the novel, Oliver arrives in London after first escaping from the workhouse and then from his work for an undertaker.

- What are the main differences you notice between this writing and more modern texts?
- What are your impressions of the two characters that feature in this extract?

OLIVER TWIST

Early on the seventh morning after he had left his native place, Oliver limped slowly into the little town of Barnet. The window-shutters were closed; the street was empty; not a soul had awakened to the business of the day. The sun was rising in all its splendid beauty; but the light only served to show the boy his own lonesomeness and desolation, as he sat, with bleeding feet and covered with dust, upon a door-step.

By degrees, the shutters were opened; the window-blinds were drawn up; and people began passing to and fro. Some few stopped to gaze at Oliver for a moment or two, or turned round to stare at him as they hurried by; but none relieved him, or troubled themselves to inquire how he came there. He had no heart to beg. And there he sat.

He had been crouching on the step for some time, wondering at the great number of public-houses[1] (every other house in Barnet was a tavern, large or small), gazing listlessly at the coaches as they passed through, and thinking how strange it seemed that they could do, with ease, in a few hours, what it had taken him a whole week of courage and determination beyond his years to accomplish, when he was roused by observing that a boy, who had passed him carelessly some minutes before, had returned, and was now surveying him most earnestly from the opposite side of the way. He took little heed of this at first; but the boy remained in the same attitude of close observation so long, that Oliver raised his head, and returned his steady look. Upon this, the boy crossed over; and, walking close up to Oliver, said,

'Hullo, my covey![2] What's the row?'

The boy who addressed this inquiry to the young wayfarer,[3] was about his own age, but one of the queerest looking boys that Oliver had ever seen. He was a snub-nosed, flat-browed, common-faced boy enough; and as dirty a juvenile as one would wish to see; but he had about him all the airs and manners of a man. He was short of his age, with rather bow-legs, and little, sharp, ugly eyes. His hat was stuck on the top of his head so lightly, that it threatened to fall off every moment – and would have done so, very often, if the wearer had not had a knack of every now and then giving his head a sudden twitch, which brought it back to its old place again. He wore a man's coat, which reached nearly to his heels. He had turned the cuffs back, half-way up his arm, to get his hands out of the sleeves: apparently with the ultimate view of thrusting them into the pockets of his corduroy trousers; for there he kept them. He was, altogether, as roystering[4] and swaggering a young gentleman as ever stood four feet six, or something less, in his bluchers.[5]

'Hullo, my covey! What's the row?' said this strange young gentleman to Oliver.

'I am very hungry and tired,' replied Oliver, the tears standing in his eyes as he spoke. 'I have walked a long way. I have been walking these seven days.'

'Walking for sivin days!' said the young gentleman. 'Oh, I see. Beak's[6] order, eh? But,' he added, noticing Oliver's look of surprise, 'I suppose you don't know what a beak is, my flash com-pan-i-on.'

Oliver mildly replied, that he had always heard a bird's mouth described by the term in question.

'My eyes,[7] how green!'[8] exclaimed the young gentleman.

---

[1] inns, taverns or 'pubs'

[2] from cove, an old-fashioned slang word for man

[3] someone travelling by foot

[4] 'to roister' means to enjoy yourself in a noisy way

[5] a type of shoe

[6] magistrate: a judge in a court that deals mostly with minor offences

[7] an expression of surprise, like 'my word' or 'good gracious'

[8] gullible or inexperienced

TEXT 6

Writer Grace Hallworth grew up in the West Indies. This short story draws on the rich folklore traditions of Trinidad and Tobago, a group of islands just off the coast of South America.

- What clues does the writer give us about what might happen?
- When do you know this is going to be a ghost story?
- Does 'The Guitarist' remind you of any other ghost stories you've read or heard?

The Guitarist

Joe was always in demand for the Singings, or community evenings held in villages which were too far away from the city to enjoy its attractions. He was an excellent guitarist, and when he wasn't performing on his own, he accompanied the singers and dancers who also attended the Singing.

After a Singing someone was sure to offer Joe a lift back to his village but on one occasion he found himself stranded miles away from his home with no choice but to set out on foot. It was a dark night and there wasn't a soul to be seen on the road, not even a cat or a dog, so Joe began to strum his guitar to hearten himself for the lonely journey ahead.

Joe had heard many stories about strange things seen at night on that road but he told himself that most of the people who related these stories had been drinking heavily. All the same, as he came to a crossroad known to be the haunt of Lajables[1] and other restless spirits, he strummed his guitar loudly to drown out the rising clamour of fearful thoughts in his head. In the quiet of early morning the tune was sharp and strong, and Joe began to move to the rhythm; but all the while his eyes were fixed on a point ahead of him where four roads met. The nearer he got, the more convinced he was that someone was standing in the middle of the road. He hoped with all his heart that he was wrong and that the shape was only a shadow cast by an overhanging tree.

The man stood so still he might have been a statue, and it was only when Joe was within arm's length of the figure that he saw any sign of life. The man was quite tall, and so thin that his clothes hung on him as though they were thrown over a wire frame. There was a musty smell about them. It was too dark to see who the man was or what he looked like, and when he spoke his voice had a rasp to it which set Joe's teeth on edge.

'You play a real fine guitar for a youngster,' said the man, falling into step beside Joe.

Just a little while before, Joe would have given anything to meet another being but somehow he was not keen to have this man as a companion. Nevertheless his motto was 'Better to be safe than sorry' so he was as polite as his unease would allow.

'It's nothing special, but I like to keep my hand in. What about you, man? Can you play guitar too?' asked Joe.

'Let me try your guitar and we'll see if I can match you,' replied the man. Joe handed over his guitar and the man began to play so gently and softly that Joe had to listen closely to hear the tune. He had never heard such a mournful air. But soon the music changed. The tune became wild and the rhythm fast and there was a harshness about it which drew a response from every nerve in Joe's body. Suddenly there was a new tune and the music became light and enchanting. Joe felt as if he were borne in the air like a blown-up balloon. He was floating on a current of music and would follow it to the ends of the earth and beyond.

And then the music stopped. Joe came back down to earth with a shock as he realized that he was standing in front of his house. The night clouds were slowly dispersing. The man handed the guitar back to Joe who was still dazed.

'Man, that was guitar like I never heard in this world before,' said Joe.

'True.' said the man. 'You should have heard me when I was alive!'

---

[1] also known as La Diablesse, a sinister female folklore figure who has odd feet – one human and one a hoof

Gulliver's Travels, first published in 1726, has never been out of print. Jonathan Swift uses his fictional traveller, Lemuel Gulliver, to make fun of human nature and 18th-century society. In this extract, Gulliver describes how he is woken from sleep by a group of tiny humans.

- What clues can you find to assess the narrator? Is he likeable? Honest? Silly? Optimistic?
- Which aspects of human nature and society do you think Swift is drawing attention to? How does he make fun of them?

Gulliver's
Travels

I was extremely tired, and with that, and the heat of the weather, and about half a pint of brandy that I drank as I left the ship, I found myself much inclined to sleep. I lay down on the grass, which was very short and soft, where I slept sounder than ever I remembered to have done in my life, and, as I reckoned, above nine hours; for when I awaked, it was just daylight. I attempted to rise, but was not able to stir, for, as I happened to lie on my back, I found my arms and legs were strongly fastened on each side to the ground, and my hair, which was long and thick, tied down in the same manner. I likewise felt several slender ligatures across my body, from my arm-pits to my thighs. I could only look upwards; the sun began to grow hot, and the light offended my eyes. I heard a confused noise about me, but in the posture I lay, could see nothing except the sky. In a little time I felt something alive moving on my left leg, which advancing gently forward over my breast, came almost up to my chin, and on bending my eyes downwards as much as I could, I perceived it to be a human creature not six inches high, with a bow and arrow in his hands, and a quiver at his back. In the meantime, I felt at least forty more of the same kind (as I conjectured) following the first. I was in the utmost astonishment, and roared so loud, that they all ran back in a fright, and some of them, as I was afterwards told, were hurt with the falls they got by leaping from my sides upon the ground. However, they soon returned, and one of them, who ventured so far as to get a full sight ▷

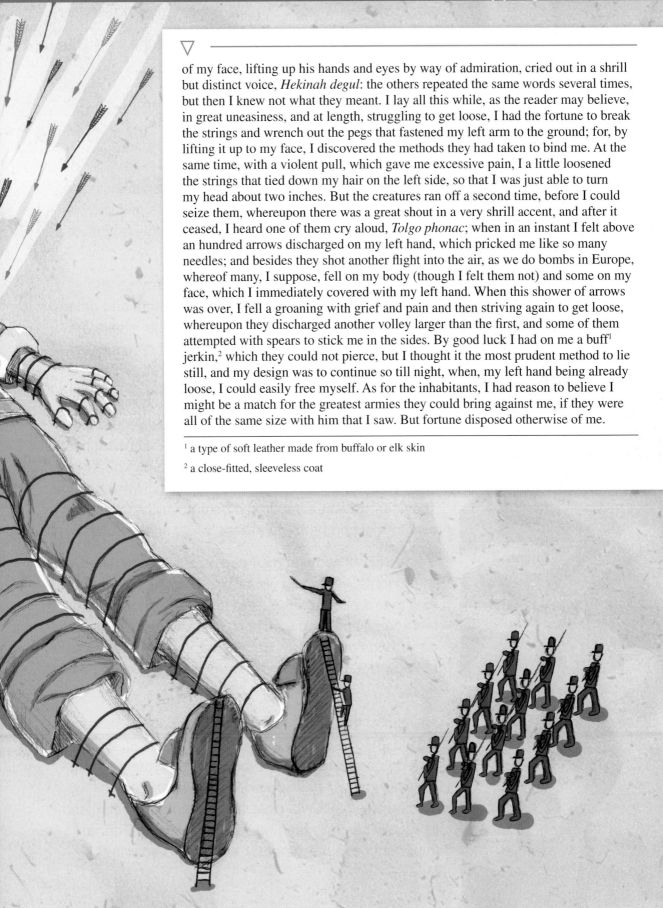

▽

of my face, lifting up his hands and eyes by way of admiration, cried out in a shrill but distinct voice, *Hekinah degul*: the others repeated the same words several times, but then I knew not what they meant. I lay all this while, as the reader may believe, in great uneasiness, and at length, struggling to get loose, I had the fortune to break the strings and wrench out the pegs that fastened my left arm to the ground; for, by lifting it up to my face, I discovered the methods they had taken to bind me. At the same time, with a violent pull, which gave me excessive pain, I a little loosened the strings that tied down my hair on the left side, so that I was just able to turn my head about two inches. But the creatures ran off a second time, before I could seize them, whereupon there was a great shout in a very shrill accent, and after it ceased, I heard one of them cry aloud, *Tolgo phonac*; when in an instant I felt above an hundred arrows discharged on my left hand, which pricked me like so many needles; and besides they shot another flight into the air, as we do bombs in Europe, whereof many, I suppose, fell on my body (though I felt them not) and some on my face, which I immediately covered with my left hand. When this shower of arrows was over, I fell a groaning with grief and pain and then striving again to get loose, whereupon they discharged another volley larger than the first, and some of them attempted with spears to stick me in the sides. By good luck I had on me a buff[1] jerkin,[2] which they could not pierce, but I thought it the most prudent method to lie still, and my design was to continue so till night, when, my left hand being already loose, I could easily free myself. As for the inhabitants, I had reason to believe I might be a match for the greatest armies they could bring against me, if they were all of the same size with him that I saw. But fortune disposed otherwise of me.

[1] a type of soft leather made from buffalo or elk skin

[2] a close-fitted, sleeveless coat

19

The many possibilities of poetry

Introduction

Poetry is everywhere: in song lyrics, advertising jingles, nursery rhymes and birthday cards. Some of it you will like, some you won't and there are probably poems that you remember parts of.

You will know by now that some poems rhyme and others don't. Some have a very clear rhythm and others seem to be free-flowing. Some are serious, others are funny. Some are easy to understand and others seem mysterious. Some are short, like haikus; others are very long indeed.

Poems are incredibly varied, as is their content. One poem might tell a story, another a joke. One poem might be a plea for equality, another might be a personal memory. And of course, poets like to play with language. They can write in a hundred different ways – from the very formal and patterned to the weird and wonderful.

Here, you will come across poems of all these types. As with people, some you will take to straight away, others may take a bit of getting used to – and some you might feel you can't get on with at all. But, as with people, don't judge too quickly. Some poems take a while to get to know but then you end up appreciating them all the more.

The aim of this unit is to improve your English skills but *also* to encourage you to write poetry yourself, and to pick up poems to read for your own enjoyment. Along the way, you will develop skills in close and careful reading (seeing how a poet has crafted the writing) and in equally carefully crafting your own writing. This is important because in poetry, every word counts.

TEXT 1

The lion dance is performed in Chinese communities on many occasions, especially Chinese New Year. 'Gong she fah chai' is 'Happy New Year' in Mandarin Chinese. This poem by Trevor Millum becomes quiet in the middle and then reaches a noisy climax.

- Notice the rhythm of the poem. How many beats are there in each line?
- Is this more of a chant than a poem? Is there a difference?

Lion Dance

Drum drum gong drum
gong gong cymbal gong
gong she fah chai
cymbal clang drum clash
gong she fah chai
lion saunter lion strut
gong-she gong-she
yellow body bright eye
gong she fah chai
eye wink eye flash
cymbal clang drum clash
lion coy lion cute
she-she she-she
lion lie lion sleep
fah chai fah chai
fah chai fah chai
gong she fah chai

man walk man creep
gong she fah chai
lion wake! lion leap!
gong she fah chai
lion angry lion cross
gong-gong she-she fah-fah chai-chai
lion leap lion high
chai! chai! chai! chai!
people cower people fly
gong chai! gong chai!
lion pounce lion prance!
gong gong gong gong gong gong gong gong
gong she fah chai!
gong gong gong gong gong gong gong gong
GONG SHE LION DANCE!!
GONG SHE LION DANCE!!

This is usually seen as a love poem from W.B. Yeats to Maud Gonne, with whom he fell in love but who turned down his many proposals of marriage. The poet would like to offer expensive gifts but cannot afford to, and so offers his precious dreams instead.

- When reading this aloud, where would you pause?
  Could you wait for the fifth line, where the main verb is?
- Does this poem rhyme?

HE WISHES FOR THE CLOTHS OF HEAVEN

Had I the heavens' embroidered cloths,

Enwrought[1] with golden and silver light,

The blue and the dim and the dark cloths

Of night and light and the half-light;

I would spread the cloths under your feet:

But I, being poor, have only my dreams;

I have spread my dreams under your feet;

Tread softly because you tread on my dreams.

---

[1] embroidered, decorated

TEXT 3

'Half Caste' contains John Agard's reflections on being of mixed race, using humour as a tool to point out the foolishness of people who use the term. It is a poem crying out to be performed.

- The poem uses non-Standard English. Does that make it hard to understand? Are there any words you don't understand until you read them aloud?
- Is it right to use the term 'rap' to describe Agard's poem?

Half Caste

Excuse me
standing on one leg
I'm half-caste

Explain yuself
wha yu mean
when yu say half-caste
yu mean when picasso
mix red an green
is a half-caste canvas/
explain yuself
wha u mean
when yu say half-caste
yu mean when light an shadow
mix in de sky
is a half-caste weather/
well in dat case
england weather
nearly always half-caste
in fact some o dem cloud
half-caste till dem overcast
so spiteful dem dont want de sun pass
ah rass/
explain yuself
wha yu mean
when yu say half-caste
yu mean tchaikovsky
sit down at dah piano
an mix a black key
wid a white key
is a half-caste symphony/

Explain yuself
wha yu mean
Ah listening to yu wid de keen
half of mih ear
Ah lookin at yu wid de keen
half of mih eye
and when I'm introduced to yu
I'm sure you'll understand
why I offer yu half-a-hand
an when I sleep at night
I close half-a-eye
consequently when I dream
I dream half-a-dream
an when moon begin to glow
I half-caste human being
cast half-a-shadow
but yu come back tomorrow
wid de whole of yu eye
an de whole of yu ear
and de whole of yu mind

an I will tell yu
de other half
of my story

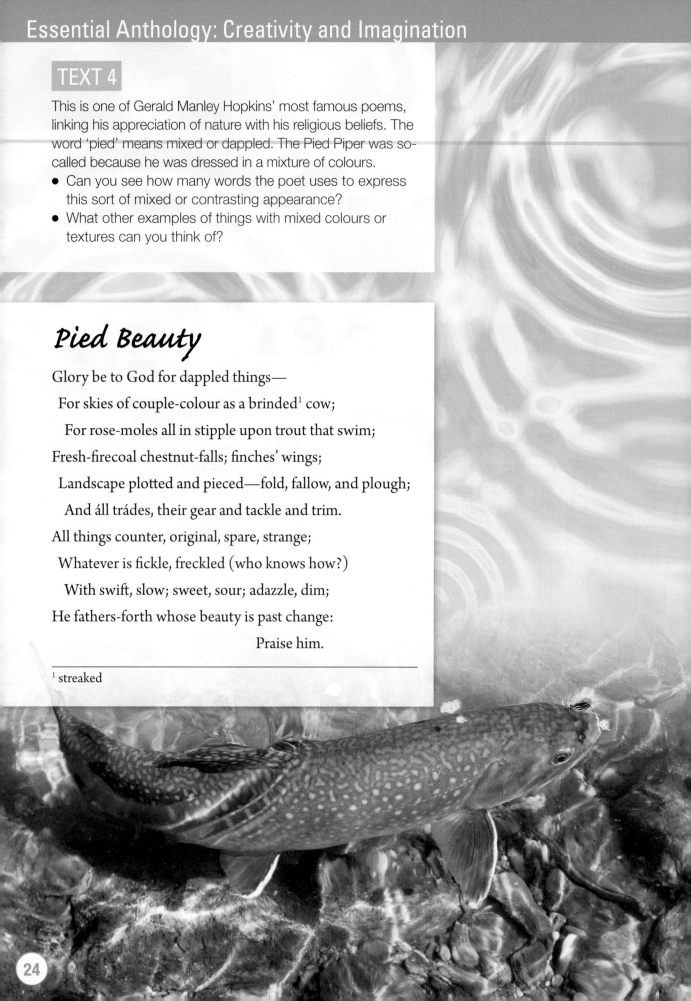

TEXT 4

This is one of Gerald Manley Hopkins' most famous poems, linking his appreciation of nature with his religious beliefs. The word 'pied' means mixed or dappled. The Pied Piper was so-called because he was dressed in a mixture of colours.

- Can you see how many words the poet uses to express this sort of mixed or contrasting appearance?
- What other examples of things with mixed colours or textures can you think of?

Pied Beauty

Glory be to God for dappled things—
  For skies of couple-colour as a brinded[1] cow;
    For rose-moles all in stipple upon trout that swim;
Fresh-firecoal chestnut-falls; finches' wings;
  Landscape plotted and pieced—fold, fallow, and plough;
    And áll trádes, their gear and tackle and trim.
All things counter, original, spare, strange;
  Whatever is fickle, freckled (who knows how?)
    With swift, slow; sweet, sour; adazzle, dim;
He fathers-forth whose beauty is past change:
                    Praise him.

[1] streaked

TEXT 5

TEXT 5

Gina Douthwaite is a children's poet who has written numerous shape poems. The poem is shown here in a more conventional way. Notice how the poem plays with language as well as shape.

- Can you imagine how this might be written as a shape?
- How would you pronounce 'rhinoceroses' in this poem?

Rhino

When more than one rhinoceros becomes rhinoceroses,

and each of these has horns of hair that stick up from their noses,

and armoured skin that wallows in the mud when they reposes,[1]

and on each foot each rhino has three hooves instead of toeses

– the features of these creatures show the problem language poses

when more than one rhinoceros becomes rhinoceroses.

---

[1] sleep

TEXT 6

Lemn Sissay was the official poet of the 2012 London Olympics. A number of his poems are displayed on buildings, like the one here. The Mancunian Way is a dual carriageway in Manchester (and a song by Take That).

- Does the pictorial arrangement of letters make the poem hard to read? Does it help to make it look like rain?
- There's no punctuation in the poem. Does it matter? How do you know where to pause?

Rain

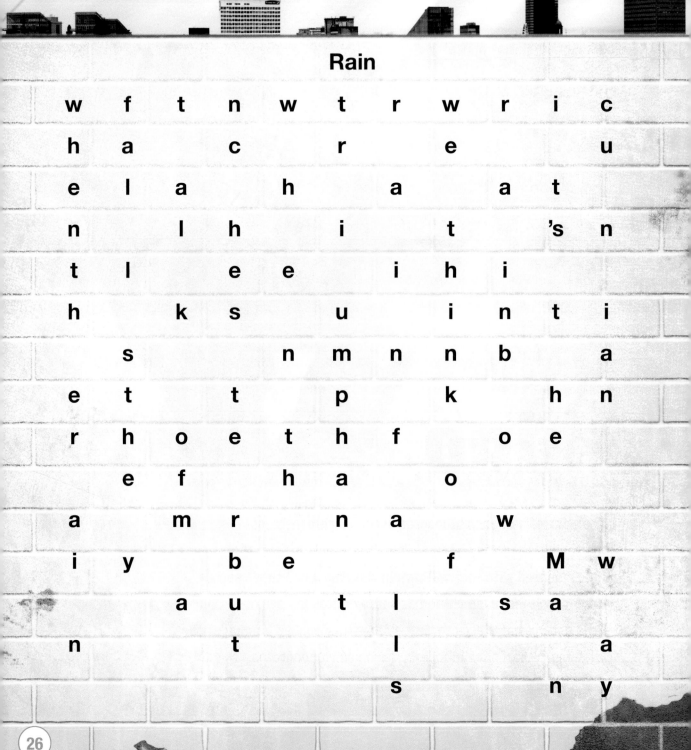

```
w   f   t   n   w   t   r   w   r   i   c
h   a   c       r       e               u
e   l   a       h       a           a   t
n   l   h       i       t          's   n
t   l   e   e       i   h       i
h   k   s       u       i   n   t   i
    s       n   m   n   n   b       a
e   t       t   p       k       h   n
r   h   o   e   t   h   f       o   e
    e   f       h   a       o
a       m   r   n   a       w
i   y       b   e       f       M   w
    a   u       t   l       s   a
n       t       l               a
                s           n   y
```

E.E. Cummings was known for his unusual use of punctuation and layout on the page, as well as the playful use (and misuse) of words and word order.

- Is this a dream, a hallucination, a real description – or what?
- What difference does the unusual layout make to your reading of the text?

The
Sky
Was

the
    sky
       was
can   dy   lu
minous
       edible
spry
     pinks shy
lemons
greens   coo l choc
olate
s.

  un der,
  a lo
  co
  mo
    tive   s pout
       ing
        vi
        o
       lets

TEXT 8

Barrie Wade's poem tells the story of a boy who is helping his friend to carry out a remembrance ceremony for his dead relations. The ceremony is known as Obon and is part of the Buddhist religion.

- Is this a sad poem – or more than that?
- What is the attitude of the writer of the poem to what's going on?

The Visitors

'Twenty-seven lamps is what it takes,' he said,
setting his little candles on the stairs,
'to light the way and welcome back the dead.'
I helped him light their little welcome flares

because he's my best mate. His Dad and Mum
were Buddhists and I know his Obon feast
means food set out for visitors to come
seeking Nirvana which, he says, is peace.

'At Obon we invite them to return
and visit us.' He paused with eyes alight –
like mine, I guess, on Christmas Eve, when wine
is left for Santa Claus. 'They'll come tonight.'

I know his grandad and his mother drowned,
with nearly everybody from their junk,
under the China Seas when bandits rammed
their overcrowded boat. He would have sunk

but for his dad and sister who took turns
to hold him up. I reckon one who's
rescued from a hell like that soon learns
what welcome lights we can't afford to lose.

'We'll burn the paper lantern now,' he said.
'Grandad used to make them out of lotus
leaves, but this will have to do instead.'
I pray and hope it helps them reach us

in these flats. I watch his eyes go still and wide
with peaceful welcome. In the flickering glare
his face is like a beacon lit to guide
the old man and his daughter up the stair.

Michael Donaghy was an Irish-American poet and musician who lived in London. This poem is a meditation on time and space, which is brought down to human level by its matter-of-fact tone.
- What is usually meant by the phrase 'for the present'?
- Who do you think this poem is written for?

The Present

For the present there is just one moon,
though every level pond gives back another.

But the bright disc shining in the black lagoon,
perceived[1] by astrophysicist and lover,

is milliseconds old. And even that light's
seven minutes older than its source.

And the stars we think we see on moonless nights
are long extinguished. And, of course,

this very moment, as you read this line,
is literally gone before you know it.

Forget the here-and-now. We have no time
but this device of wantoness[2] and wit.

Make me this present then: your hand in mine,
and we'll live out our lives in it.

[1] noticed
[2] literally immorality but here more to do
with carefreeness, freedom

TEXT 10

John Clare was a self-taught poet of the 19th century, with very little formal education. He is well known for his nature poetry. He suffered mental health problems and 'I Am' is almost certainly based on personal experience.

- How many negative words can you find – like 'none' or 'lost'? Are there any positive ones?
- Why might someone write a poem like this – and for whom?

I Am

I am – yet what I am, none cares or knows;
    My friends forsake me like a memory lost: –
I am the self-consumer of my woes; –
    They rise and vanish in oblivion's host,
Like shadows in love's frenzied stifled throes: –
And yet I am, and live – like vapours tossed

Into the nothingness of scorn and noise, –
    Into the living sea of waking dreams,
Where there is neither sense of life or joys,
    But the vast shipwreck of my life's esteems;
Even the dearest, that I love the best
Are strange – nay, rather stranger than the rest.

I long for scenes, where man hath never trod,
    A place where woman never smiled or wept,
There to abide with my Creator, God;
    And sleep as I in childhood, sweetly slept,
Untroubling, and untroubled where I lie,
The grass below – above the vaulted sky.

TEXT 11

Bernard Young is a children's poet who is widely anthologised, runs school workshops and likes cats. You can find a performance of his poem on YouTube.

- Is this a song or a poem? What's the difference?
- Can you find other examples of poems where writers put themselves in the position of animals?

I'm a Cat

I'm a cat
an ordinary cat
it's so simple
simple as that

That I'm a cat
an ordinary cat
and I do what cats do

I like to stare
and drink from a tap
I like to purr
when I'm sitting on a lap
I use my litter
when I need to poo
I do what cats do

But when I dream
I dream of mice
and I think
just how nice
it would be
if I could play
with them *Yum! Yum!*

But when he dreams
he dreams of love
he looks to the sky above
he seems confused
as if he's in a daze

But he's a man
an ordinary man
doing the best he can

It's not enough
it never is
but he's doing the best he can

But when I dream
I dream of birds
and I won't
mince my words
I would like
to get my claws
on them *Yum! Yum!*

I'm a cat
an ordinary cat
it's so simple
simple as that

That I'm a cat
an ordinary cat
and I do what cats do
I do what cats
I do what cats ... do!

TEXT 12

Henry Beard is an American writer whose collection *Poetry for Cats* is made up of parodies of famous poems rewritten from a cat's point of view. This poem is written as if by a cat who delights in breaking things.

- 'To a Vase' is based on a poem called 'How Do I Love Thee?' See if you can find the original and compare it to this version.
- Can you find other examples of parodies?

To a Vase

How do I break thee? Let me count the ways.

I break thee if thou art at any height

My paw can reach, when, smarting from some slight,

I sulk, or have one of my crazy days.

I break thee with an accidental graze

Or twitch of tail, if I should take a fright.

I break thee out of pure and simple spite

The way I broke the jar of mayonnaise.

I break thee if a bug upon thee sits.

I break thee if I'm in a playful mood,

And then I wrestle with the shiny bits.

I break thee if I do not like my food.

And if someone thy shards[1] together fits,

I'll break thee once again when thou art glued.

---

[1] pieces, usually of pottery

TEXT 13

'The Nightmare' is an extract from a comic opera called *Iolanthe*. W.S. Gilbert was famous for his clever lyrics and wordplay, and these were set to music by Arthur Sullivan, creating the famous Gilbert and Sullivan partnership.

- Can you work out the rhythm to which the words might be sung? Try tapping it out – is it regular?
- Some of the vocabulary might be unfamiliar. See if you can work out the meaning of these words before you look for their definitions at the bottom.

THE NIGHTMARE

When you're lying awake
with a dismal headache,
and repose is tabooed[1] by anxiety,
I conceive you may use
any language you choose
to indulge in without impropriety;[2]

For your brain is on fire
– the bedclothes conspire[3]
of usual slumber to plunder you:[4]
First your counterpane[5] goes
and uncovers your toes,
and your sheet slips demurely from under you;

Then the blanketing tickles –
you feel like mixed pickles –
so terribly sharp is the pricking,
And you're hot, and you're cross,
and you tumble and toss
till there's nothing 'twixt you and the ticking.[6]

Then the bedclothes all creep
to the ground in a heap,
and you pick 'em all up in a tangle;
Next your pillow resigns
and politely declines
to remain at its usual angle!
Well, you get some repose
in the form of a doze,
with hot eyeballs and head ever aching,
But your slumbering teems

with such horrible dreams
that you'd very much better be waking;
[…]
You're a regular wreck,
with a crick in your neck,
and no wonder you snore,
for your head's on the floor,
and you've needles and pins
from your soles to your shins,
and your flesh is a-creep,
for your left leg's asleep,
and you've cramp in your toes,
and a fly on your nose,
and some fluff in your lung,
and a feverish tongue,
and a thirst that's intense,
and a general sense
that you haven't been sleeping in clover;
But the darkness has passed,
and it's daylight at last,
and the night has been long –
ditto, ditto my song –
and thank goodness they're both of them over!

---

[1] forbidden
[2] wrongdoing
[3] plot or plan
[4] take away from you
[5] bed covering
[6] mattress stuffing

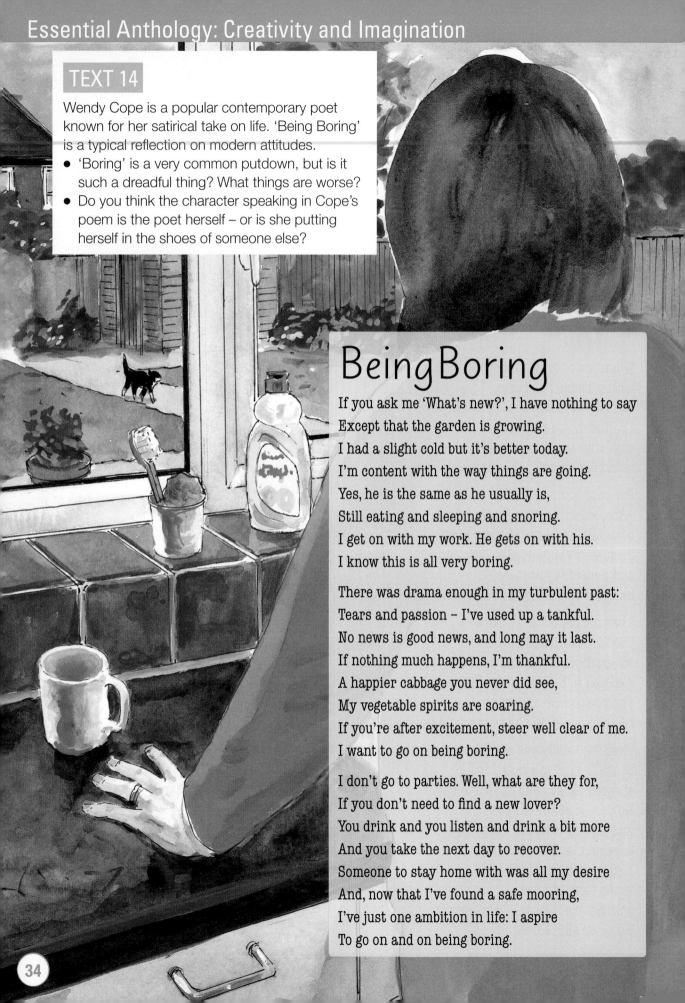

TEXT 14

Wendy Cope is a popular contemporary poet known for her satirical take on life. 'Being Boring' is a typical reflection on modern attitudes.

- 'Boring' is a very common putdown, but is it such a dreadful thing? What things are worse?
- Do you think the character speaking in Cope's poem is the poet herself – or is she putting herself in the shoes of someone else?

Being Boring

If you ask me 'What's new?', I have nothing to say
Except that the garden is growing.
I had a slight cold but it's better today.
I'm content with the way things are going.
Yes, he is the same as he usually is,
Still eating and sleeping and snoring.
I get on with my work. He gets on with his.
I know this is all very boring.

There was drama enough in my turbulent past:
Tears and passion – I've used up a tankful.
No news is good news, and long may it last.
If nothing much happens, I'm thankful.
A happier cabbage you never did see,
My vegetable spirits are soaring.
If you're after excitement, steer well clear of me.
I want to go on being boring.

I don't go to parties. Well, what are they for,
If you don't need to find a new lover?
You drink and you listen and drink a bit more
And you take the next day to recover.
Someone to stay home with was all my desire
And, now that I've found a safe mooring,
I've just one ambition in life: I aspire
To go on and on being boring.

TEXT 15

This is one of Rudyard Kipling's best-known poems. The description appears realistic but there are also some dreamlike or ghostly images depicted.

- Is this a poem about ghosts – or just about memories?
- How do you think the poet came to write this? If they shut the road 70 years ago, how does he know about it? Do you think it's a real road the poet heard about or something he invented?

The Way Through the Woods

They shut the road through the woods
Seventy years ago.
Weather and rain have undone it again,
And now you would never know
There was once a road through the woods
Before they planted the trees.
It is underneath the coppice and heath,
And the thin anemones.
Only the keeper sees
That, where the ring-dove broods,
And the badgers roll at ease,
There was once a road through the woods.

Yet, if you enter the woods
Of a summer evening late,
When the night-air cools on the trout-ringed pools
Where the otter whistles his mate,
(They fear not men in the woods,
Because they see so few.)
You will hear the beat of a horse's feet,
And the swish of a skirt in the dew,
Steadily cantering through
The misty solitudes,
As though they perfectly knew
The old lost road through the woods.
But there is no road through the woods.

TEXT 16

Norman MacCaig is best known for his poems about the wilds of Scotland but here he writes about New York.

- Quite a lot of the images the poet uses are taken from the popular view of the Wild West. Can you spot some of them?
- Which would be more dangerous for a stranger, a Wild West town or New York after dark? How much do we rely on stories, films and myths to answer that?

Hotel Room, 12th Floor

This morning I watched from here
a helicopter skirting like a damaged insect
the Empire State Building, that
jumbo size dentist's drill, and landing
on the roof of the PanAm skyscraper.
But now midnight has come in
from foreign places. Its uncivilised darkness
is shot at by a million lit windows, all
ups and acrosses.

But midnight is not
so easily defeated. I lie in bed, between
a radio and a television set, and hear
the wildest of warwhoops continually ululating[1] through
the glittering canyons and gulches –
police cars and ambulances racing
to the broken bones, the harsh screaming
from coldwater flats, the blood
glazed on sidewalks.

The frontier is never
somewhere else. And no stockades
can keep the midnight out.

---
[1] wailing

East 46th St

TEXT 17

Grace Nichols comes from Guyana and lives in England. She has written a number of poems about having to live with two identities: her past and her present, her birth home and her adopted home.

- 'He always comes back …' Where is the Island Man coming back to? Where has he been?
- Which words or sounds give an idea of the waves on the beach – or the sound of the traffic?

Island Man

Morning
and island man wakes up
to the sound of blue surf
in his head
the steady breaking and wombing

wild seabirds
and fishermen pushing out to sea
the sun surfacing defiantly
from the east
of his small emerald island
he always comes back   groggily groggily

Comes back to sands
of a grey metallic soar
                         to surge of wheels
to dull North Circular roar

muffling muffling
his crumpled pillow waves
island man heaves himself

Another London day

TEXT 18

Sheenagh Pugh comes from Wales but now lives in Shetland. 'What If This Road' is suggestive and slightly surreal (dreamlike). She imagines that the road itself might decide just for once to go somewhere else.

- Where else might you find surreal ideas like this? Comedy? Science fiction?
- To whom is the poet talking?

WHAT IF THIS ROAD

What if this road, that has held no surprises
these many years, decided not to go
home after all; what if it could turn
left or right with no more ado
than a kite-tail? What if its tarry skin
were like a long, supple bolt of cloth,
that is shaken and rolled out, and takes
a new shape from the contours beneath?
And if it chose to lay itself down
in a new way; around a blind corner,
across hills you must climb without knowing
what's on the other side; who would not hanker
to be going, at all risks? Who wants to know
a story's end, or where a road will go?

Introduction

In the modern theatre with the house lights down and the stage brightly lit, it's easy to enter into the world that the playwright is presenting to us. But ever since the days of the Ancient Greeks, people have thronged to see stories performed in front of them. Today, television and film have largely replaced the theatre as the place to watch stories being acted out, but live theatre is still popular and can greatly influence our lives.

In this unit you'll read a mixture of modern scripts and texts from centuries ago. You will also notice that Shakespeare is well represented here. There's no doubt that he is widely regarded as the finest dramatist who ever lived, and it's right that we take a look at some of the scenes he wrote. We will consider why his language and stagecraft make him admired throughout the world. All the extracts in this unit were written to be performed, not simply read, and we hope that you'll take an active (and sometimes dramatic!) approach to working with them.

Writing for the stage requires special skills. In the extracts that follow, you'll see those skills well used. We hope that you'll also read the scripts with a critical eye, looking at how the writers build up character and setting, and how they draw us in to their worlds.

Reading plays is different from reading novels, short stories and poetry. The extracts in this unit will give you a flavour of the best writing for the theatre, and we hope they will encourage you to go out and become part of the audience in a theatre near you. Or, even better, you could take advantage of the many opportunities there are to get involved in acting, writing and the general putting-on of plays.

TEXT 1

This is part of the opening scene of a play called *Black Harvest* by Nigel Gray. Colin, Prill and their family have just arrived at a newly built holiday bungalow on the west coast of Ireland.

- What do you learn from this extract about the setting?
- What do you find out about the character of Oliver (even though we never see him)?
- How is the writer helping us to get to know the characters and the setting?

Black Harvest

Prill's bedroom. Day.

Colin is sitting on the edge of Prill's bed while Prill is unpacking her clothes.

Colin   I thought we were never going to get here.

Prill   Me too.

Colin   That weed, Oliver! What did we have to cart him along for?

Prill   I suppose he can't help it. It's the first time he's ever been away from his mum.

Colin   Why couldn't we have had some decent cousins? I hate kids who keep being car sick. It's bad enough with the baby and everything.

Prill   But it's nice here – now we've actually arrived.

Colin   Yeah. Smashing.

Prill	Except I was expecting an old house. Not everything brand new like this.
Colin	Dad's friend's never even been here yet. We're the first people to stay in it.
Prill	It's a bit posh though. Mum's scared Alison's going to make a mess on the carpet.
Colin	Well it's a stupid colour, cream for a carpet you've got to walk on. And it's not fair having to keep Jessie chained up outside.
Prill	But I think she'll love it here – running on the beach and everything. And my room's lovely.
Colin	Yeah. **You** don't have to share a room with that creep, Oliver.
Prill	Where is he now?
Colin	He's got his nose stuck in a book about insects or something.
Prill	Already?
Colin	He was reading about Irish history in the car.
Prill	I know.
Colin	And this is supposed to be a holiday!
Prill	Whew! I'm so hot. I thought it was always raining in Ireland.
Colin	I'll open the window.
Prill	I've tried. It's all stuck with the new paint.

Colin and Prill cross to the window. Colin tries to open it and fails. He bangs with his fist all around the frame.

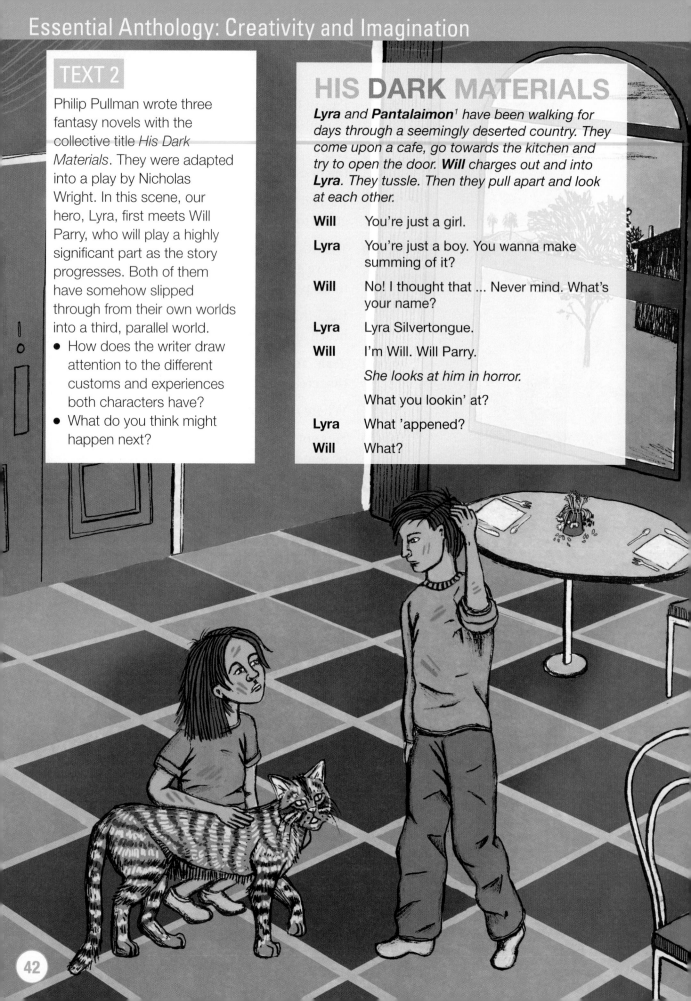

TEXT 2

Philip Pullman wrote three fantasy novels with the collective title *His Dark Materials*. They were adapted into a play by Nicholas Wright. In this scene, our hero, Lyra, first meets Will Parry, who will play a highly significant part as the story progresses. Both of them have somehow slipped through from their own worlds into a third, parallel world.

- How does the writer draw attention to the different customs and experiences both characters have?
- What do you think might happen next?

HIS DARK MATERIALS

Lyra and ***Pantalaimon***[1] *have been walking for days through a seemingly deserted country. They come upon a cafe, go towards the kitchen and try to open the door.* ***Will*** *charges out and into* ***Lyra***. *They tussle. Then they pull apart and look at each other.*

Will   You're just a girl.

Lyra   You're just a boy. You wanna make summing of it?

Will   No! I thought that ... Never mind. What's your name?

Lyra   Lyra Silvertongue.

Will   I'm Will. Will Parry.

She looks at him in horror.

What you lookin' at?

Lyra   What 'appened?

Will   What?

Lyra	Did they do it to you as well?	**Lyra**	I might.
Will	What you talkin' about?	**Will**	All right. I come from a different world.
Lyra	Your daemon! Where's your daemon?	**Lyra**	You too?
Will	My *demon*?	**Will**	What do you mean, 'you too'?
Lyra	Yeah. Like Pan.	**Lyra**	Well … So do I.
Will	I haven't got a demon. I don't *want* a demon. Are you talkin' about that cat?	**Will**	Honest?
Pantalaimon	I think he really doesn't know.	**Lyra**	Yeah.
Will	It talks!	**Will**	So ... How did you get here?
Pantalaimon	Of course I talk! Did you think I was just a pet?	**Lyra**	Through the Aurora.[2]
Will	That's incredible. A talking cat! Now I've seen everything. Is it ... Can I pat it?	**Will**	Rubbish!
Pantalaimon	No!	**Lyra**	What about you, then?
Lyra	Nobody pats another person's daemon. Never, ever.	**Will**	I came through a window in the air. Near a bus shelter in Oxford.
Will	I was trying to be nice, that's all. Where I come from, a demon is something evil, something devilish.	**Lyra**	That's impossible.
Lyra	Where is it? Where you come from?	**Will**	Yeah, and walking through the Aurora, that's just normal, I suppose. Tell you what. I'll pretend to believe you and you pretend to believe me, and then we won't have a row. All right?
Will	It ... No, you wouldn't believe it.		

[1] in Lyra's world, everyone has a daemon, an animal that is an inseparable part of a person. Pantalaimon is Lyra's daemon

[2] arches of coloured lights occurring in the night skies around the Poles

Frank Cottrell Boyce wrote a highly successful novel called *Millions*, then a play script version of the story. Two brothers, Damian and Anthony, find a bag stuffed with £200,000 in cash – the proceeds of a robbery that went wrong – but they have only 17 days to spend it all before the pound is replaced by the euro.

- How does the writer establish the differences in outlook between Damian and Anthony in this scene?
- Is Damian right to want to give the money away?

MILLIONS

Damian turns round and sees someone standing there behind him. A man in a waterproof coat, with a woollen hat pulled down around his head. He looks scary to us, but not to Damian.

[…]

Damian I'm Damian. Can I help you?

The man moves menacingly close to Damian.

Man I'm looking for money. Know anything about that?

Damian Are you poor?

Man What?

Damian Are you poor? I've got loads of money.

Man Are you trying to be funny?

He's really threatening now. But Anthony appears at the side of the stage and calls out.

Anthony Damian! Damian, Dad wants you.

Damian Sorry, got to go.

He runs down stage to Anthony while the man remains upstage. Anthony grabs Damian and whispers to him angrily.

Anthony Who's that?

Damian I'm not sure.

Anthony	He's a stranger. What has Dad told you about talking to strangers?
Damian	I think he's poor. I told him we had loads of money.
Anthony	You did what!?
Damian	What's the point of having all this money if we can't help the poor with it? That's why He gave it to us. What are you doing?
Anthony	Nothing. Nothing. Leave it to me …
	He runs off stage then comes back. Behind his back he is carrying a big bottle of pennies. He carries it over to the man and speaks to him in a simpering, goody-two-shoes voice.
Anthony	Excuse me. My little brother said you were poor …
Man	Is this some kind of wind up? Because I don't take too kindly to …
Anthony	We've got loads of money …
Man	Oh yeah?
Anthony	But we like to help the poor, so you can have it.
	He produces the bottle of coins from behind his back.
	Go on. Take it. Honestly. We want you to.

	*He forces it on the man, who takes it. Then **Anthony** runs back to **Damian**. The man wanders downstage. (…)*
Damian	Couldn't we give him a little bit more? He looked cold. Just four or five hundred.
Anthony	You've got to be more careful. The world is full of dangerous, greedy people.
Damian	The world is full of poor people and we've got a chance to help them.
Anthony	Everyone knows you shouldn't talk to strangers.
Damian	The Good Samaritan[1] was a stranger when he helped the man who'd been attacked by robbers.
Anthony	You missed the whole point of that story. That man was attacked by robbers, why? Because he was throwing his money round like an idiot. If it wasn't for the Good Samaritan he'd be dead. I'm the Good Samaritan.
Damian	But we must have been given this money for a reason …

---

[1] in the Bible, Jesus tells the story of a Jew who is beaten and robbed. A Samaritan goes out of his way to help him. Traditionally Samaritans and Jews were fierce enemies

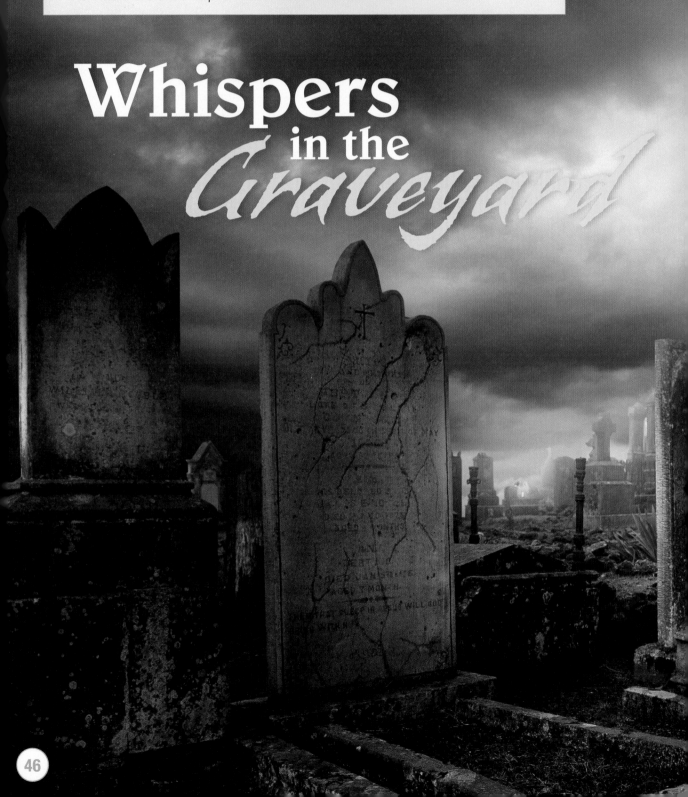

TEXT 4

Whispers in the Graveyard was originally a novel by Theresa Breslin. In the play version by Richard Conlon, the writer uses the unusual idea of the gravestones as a chorus, helping the audience to visualise what is happening and sometimes commenting on the action which here is reaching a climax.

- In this extract, how do the stones help the staging?
- How do the stones help to build dramatic tension in the audience?

Whispers
in the
Graveyard

*The **Stones** take up their positions. **Amy** sits centre, in darkness.*

STONE 1 There is a storm coming.

STONE 2 The rush of black water in the river.

STONE 3 The wind in the blurred outline of trees.

STONE 4 The sky darkens. The clouds gather, obscure the pale moon.

STONE 5 And in the darkness something is moving.

STONE 6 He is coming.

STONE 1 He is running through the night and through brambles, thorns pulling at his flesh.

STONE 2 His breath is rasping in his lungs. Feet slide on leaf-slip black soil.

STONE 3 He sees the solid wooden fence, not broken but blasted and torn aside like so many twigs.

STONE 4 Space enough for a child to pass through.

STONE 5 But he hears no whispers in his head now – the voices are quieted.

STONE 6 For the girl is in the graveyard – and Malefice[1] has what Malefice wants.

Solomon runs on, stands to one side, looks about him.

SOLOMON (*A panicked, harsh whisper.*) Amy … Amy!?

He moves off again.

STONE 6 Through and through, and on and on.

STONE 5 Hands torn by twisted, toothed wire.

STONE 4 Splinters under bloodied skin.

STONE 3 Follow the stench.

STONE 2 Towards the foul earth.

STONE 1 The ancient rot and stain.

*Solomon enters, sees **Amy**.*

SOLOMON Amy, Amy, it's me, Solomon.

AMY (*Transfixed, not looking at Solomon.*) Look Solomon. I heard the lady calling me and I got out of bed and I came, and I knew to come here *and I found this*. See what I've got, sweeties – and such pretty things, beads. Pretty beads.

SOLOMON (*Trying to warn her without scaring her.*) No, Amy, you're wrong. They're just pebbles. It's just dirt – nothing more.

MALEFICE (*As many voices, off.*) But look, Solomon, look closer. Not pebbles, not even pretty glass beads, but more valuable. Do you see?

SOLOMON (*Haltingly.*) Yes.

MALEFICE Treasure, Solomon.

SOLOMON Not glass beads, Amy.

SOLOMON/MALEFICE Diamonds, rubies, emeralds.

MALEFICE The answer to all your wishes. Imagine it! To be rich – very, very rich.

AMY (*Holding out her hand.*) Do you want one? The pink ones are my favourites.

SOLOMON (*Finding a strength from within him.*) This is wrong. Amy, look at me. Look at me and hear what I'm saying. There is something bad here, and it's in our heads. It's telling you that you have pretty beads and sweeties, and it's telling me that I've found treasure – telling me that I'll be rich.

AMY Treasure?

SOLOMON But it's a lie, Amy. Not real. *Not real.* Feel what you have in your hand Amy, trust what you feel.

---

[1] in this play, an evil character; the word itself is ancient, and means witch

TEXT 5

One of the most famous monsters in fiction comes from Mary Shelley's novel *Frankenstein*. Most people imagine that this is the name of the monster, but in fact Frankenstein is the doctor who put together the monster and brought it to life. In this extract from the play version by Philip Pullman, the monster has killed Frankenstein's young brother, and begins to explain why.

- Why do you think the monster has gone from experiencing everything as new and beautiful to murdering a child?
- Why can the monster 'never be happy'?

FRANKENSTEIN   Monster! I didn't create you to do evil – why have you betrayed me?

MONSTER   I – betray you? If I knew how to laugh, Frankenstein, I'd shake the house with scorn. *You* are the betrayer – you created me and you made sure I could never be happy. Isn't that betrayal?

FRANKENSTEIN   No! I swear it wasn't like that. I made you, yes –

MONSTER   And as soon as you saw what you'd done, you turned away in horror and left me to find my own way through the world – a creature everyone turned from with disgust and loathing – a vision from a nightmare! But do you know the cruellest thing of all? It was that I wanted to love. I came to life full of goodwill and friendship for every living creature – I wanted to help and protect them and give them all the love I felt for them – and when I tried, they stoned me and shot me and set their dogs on me – and even the dogs turned away in disgust ... Frankenstein, has any man in history ever been more cruel than you have been to me?

FRANKENSTEIN   You killed my little brother! Is that love? Is that goodwill?

MONSTER   Listen! And I'll tell you everything.

He releases Frankenstein, who falls into the chair. The Monster walks up and down as he speaks; Frankenstein hides his head in his hands, occasionally looking up to reply – the very picture of despair.

When I came to life I knew nothing. I didn't know who I was, I didn't know what the world was – things had no names. The only thing I knew was pain, but I didn't know what that was till much later, when I found out what it was called. Everything was new, Frankenstein. Do you know how beautiful things are when they're new? Or have you forgotten?

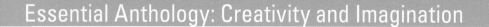

TEXT 6

Romeo and Juliet is one of William Shakespeare's best-loved plays. In this extract, Romeo has gatecrashed a big party that is being thrown by the Capulet family. It is here that he first sets eyes on Juliet – and instantly falls in love with her.

- How does Shakespeare make it clear that this is love at first sight?
- How does he indicate to the audience that tragedy is only just below the surface of this lovers' meeting?

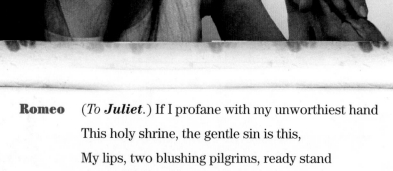

Romeo	(*To **Juliet**.*) If I profane with my unworthiest hand
	This holy shrine, the gentle sin is this,
	My lips, two blushing pilgrims, ready stand
	To smooth that rough touch with a tender kiss.
Juliet	Good pilgrim, you do wrong your hand too much,
	Which mannerly devotion shows in this;
	For saints have hands that pilgrims' hands do touch,
	And palm to palm is holy palmers'[1] kiss.

Romeo	Have not saints lips, and holy palmers too?
Juliet	Ay pilgrim, lips that they must use in prayer.
Romeo	O then dear saint, let lips do what hands do.
	They pray; grant thou, lest faith turn to despair.
Juliet	Saints do not move, though grant for prayers' sake.
Romeo	Then move not, while my prayer's effect I take.
	Kisses her.
	Thus from my lips, by thine, my sin is purged.
Juliet	Then have my lips the sin that they have took.
Romeo	Sin from thy lips? O trespass sweetly urged.
	Give me my sin again.
Juliet	You kiss by th' book.
Nurse	Madam, your mother craves a word with you.
Romeo	What is her mother?
Nurse	Marry,[2] bachelor,
	Her mother is the lady of the house,
	And a good lady, and a wise and virtuous.
	I nursed her daughter, that you talked withal;
	I tell you, he that can lay hold of her
	Shall have the chinks.[3]
Romeo	Is she a Capulet?[4]
	O dear account, my life is my foe's debt.
Benvolio	Away, be gone, the sport is at the best.
Romeo	Ay, so I fear; the more is my unrest.

---

[1] pilgrim

[2] not used in the modern sense. Here it means, 'Well, of course …'

[3] money

[4] one of the leading families in Verona. The other leading family was the Montagues and there was bitter rivalry between the two. Juliet is a Capulet; Romeo is a Montague

TEXT 7

In Shakespeare's *The Tempest*, Prospero, the Duke of Milan, was forced out by Alonso to live on a remote island with his daughter, Miranda. Using his magic, Prospero created a shipwreck that brought Alonso and his son, Ferdinand, to the island. Alonso believes that his son drowned, but in fact Prospero has arranged for him to meet and fall in
love with Miranda. Here Prospero reveals what he has done.

- Can you identify what each of the speakers is feeling as the scene unfolds?
- Are Prospero's actions right or wrong?

THE
TEMPEST

Prospero	For you, most wicked sir, whom to call brother
	Would even infect my mouth, I do forgive
	Thy rankest fault – all of them – and require
	My Dukedom of thee, which perforce[1] I know,
	Thou must restore.
Alonso	If thou be'st Prospero,
	Give us particulars of thy preservation,
	How thou hast met us here, who three hours since
	Were wracked upon this shore? where I have lost –
	How sharp the point of this remembrance is –
	My dear son Ferdinand.

Prospero	I am woe for't, sir.
Alonso	Irreparable is the loss, and Patience
	Says it is past her cure.
Prospero	I rather think
	You have not sought her help, of whose soft grace
	For the like loss,[2] I have her sovereign aid
	And rest myself content.
Alonso	You the like loss?
Prospero	As great to me, as late; and, supportable
	To make the dear loss, have I means much weaker
	Than you may call to comfort you; for I
	Have lost my daughter.
Alonso	A daughter?
	O heavens, that they were living both in Naples,
	The King and Queen there! That they were, I wish
	Myself were mudded in that oozy bed
	Where my son lies. When did you lose your daughter?
Prospero	In this last tempest. I perceive these lords
	At this encounter do so much admire
	That they devour their reason and scarce think
	Their eyes do offices of truth, their words
	Are natural breath; but howsoe'er you have
	Been jostled from your senses, know for certain
	That I am Prospero and that very Duke
	Which was thrust forth of Milan; who most strangely
	Upon this shore, where you were wracked, was landed,
	To be the lord on't. No more yet of this,
	For 'tis a chronicle of day by day,
	Not a relation for a breakfast, nor
	Befitting this first meeting. Welcome, sir;
	This cell's my court; here have I few attendants,
	And subjects none abroad. Pray you, look in.
	My Dukedom since you have given me again,
	I will requite you with as good a thing,
	At least bring forth a wonder, to content ye
	As much as me my Dukedom.

*Here **Prospero** discovers **Ferdinand** and **Miranda**
playing at chess.*

Miranda	Sweet lord, you play me false.
Ferdinand	No, my dearest love,
	I would not for the world.
Miranda	Yes, for a score of kingdoms, you should wrangle,
	And I would call it fair play.

---

[1] you cannot avoid
[2] a similar bereavement

Alonso	If this prove
	A vision of the island, one dear son
	Shall I twice lose.
Sebastian	A most high miracle.
Ferdinand	*Having seen **Alonso**.*
	Though the seas threaten, they are merciful;
	I have cursed them without cause.
	*Kneels before **Alonso**.*
Alonso	Now all the blessings
	Of a glad father compass³ thee about!
	Arise, and say how thou cam'st here.
Miranda	O, wonder!
	How many goodly creatures are there here!
	How beauteous mankind is! O brave new world
	That has such people in't!

---

³ encircle. Alsonso hugs his son

TEXT 8

In this extract from *A Midsummer Night's Dream* Lysander loves Hermia, but a magic potion put on him means that he has suddenly fallen head over heels in love with Helena, Hermia's friend. Lysander hates the thought that Hermia will come between them and tries to send her away, which leads to a huge argument.

- How does Shakespeare build up the humour in this scene?
- How many different words for 'small' and 'tall' can you find?

A Midsummer Night's Dream

Hermia	What? Can you do me greater harm than hate?
	Hate me? Wherefore? O me, what news, my love?
	Am not I Hermia? Are not you Lysander?
	I am as fair now as I was erewhile.[1]
	Since night you loved me; yet since night you left me.
	Why then, you left me – O, the gods forbid! –
	In earnest, shall I say?
Lysander	Ay, by my life;
	And never did desire to see thee more.
	Therefore be out of hope, of question, of doubt –
	Be certain. Nothing truer. 'Tis no jest
	That I do hate thee, and love Helena.
Hermia	O me! (*To* **Helena**.) You juggler, you canker blossom![2]
	You thief of love! What, have you come by night
	And stol'n my love's heart from him?

[1] before
[2] a thing that ruins something beautiful

Helena	Fine, i'faith.
	Have you no modesty, no maiden shame,
	No touch of bashfulness? What, will you tear
	Impatient answers from my gentle tongue?
	Fie, fie, you counterfeit, you puppet you!
Hermia	Puppet! Why so? Ay, that way goes the game.
	Now I perceive that she hath made compare
	Between our statures. She hath urged her height,
	And with her personage, her tall personage,
	Her height, forsooth, she hath prevailed with him.
	And are you grown so high in his esteem
	Because I am so dwarfish and so low?
	How low am I, thou painted maypole? Speak!
	How low am I? I am not yet so low
	But that my nails can reach unto thine eyes.
Helena	I pray you, though you mock me, gentlemen,
	Let her not hurt me I was never curst;
	I have no gift at all in shrewishness;[3]
	I am a right maid for my cowardice.
	Let her not strike me. You perhaps may think,
	Because she is something lower than myself
	That I can match her.
Hermia	'Lower'? Hark, again!
Helena	Good Hermia, do not be so bitter with me.
	I evermore did love you, Hermia,
	Did ever keep your counsels, never wronged you;
	Save that in love unto Demetrius,
	I told him of your stealth unto this wood.
	He followed you; for love I followed him.
	But he hath chid[4] me hence, and threatened me
	To strike me, spurn me – nay, to kill me too.
	And now, so you will let me quiet go,
	To Athens will I bear my folly back
	And follow you no further. Let me go.
	You see how simple and how fond I am.

Hermia	Why, get you gone! Who is't that hinders you?
Helena	A foolish heart that I leave here behind.
Hermia	What, with Lysander?
Helena	With Demetrius.
Lysander	Be not afraid; she shall not harm thee, Helena.
Demetrius	No, sir. She shall not, though you take her part.
Helena	O, when she's angry, she is keen and shrewd.
	She was a vixen when she went to school;
	And though she be but little, she is fierce.
Hermia	'Little' again? nothing but 'low' and 'little'?
	Why will you suffer her to flout me thus?
	Let me come to her.
Lysander	Get you gone, you dwarf!
	You minimus[5] of hindering knotgrass made,
	You bead, you acorn!
Demetrius	You are too officious
	In her behalf that scorns your services.
	Let her alone. Speak not of Helena;
	Take not her part. For if thou dost intend
	Never so little show of love to her,
	Thou shalt aby[6] it.
Lysander	Now she holds me not.
	Now follow – if thou dar'st – to try whose right,
	Of thine or mine, is most in Helena.
Demetrius	Follow? Nay, I'll go with thee, cheek by jowl.[7]
	*Exeunt **Lysander** and **Demetrius**.*

[3] being argumentative or quarrelsome

[4] told (me) off

[5] extremely small person

[6] a version of 'abide' – to tolerate or withstand

[7] the hanging part of a double chin

TEXT 9

Macbeth, King of Scotland, has murdered friends and relatives, first to seize the throne and then to maintain his position as king. Now his enemies surround him and his friends desert him; a servant brings news that his wife has died, probably by suicide. Macbeth reflects on the purpose of life.

- What would you say was Macbeth's outlook at this point?
- Would many people agree with his view of what life is, and what it's for?

MACBETH

Macbeth	I have almost forgot the taste of fears.
	The time has been my senses would have cooled
	To hear a night-shriek,[1] and my fell[2] of hair
	Would at a dismal treatise[3] rouse and stir
	As life were in't. I have supped[4] full with horrors;
	Direness, familiar to my slaughterous thoughts,
	Cannot once start me.
	Re-enter **Seyton**.
	Wherefore was that cry?
Seyton	The Queen, my lord, is dead.
Macbeth	She should have died hereafter;
	There would have been a time for such a word.
	Tomorrow, and tomorrow, and tomorrow,
	Creeps in this petty pace from day to day,
	To the last syllable of recorded time;
	And all our yesterdays have lighted fools
	The way to dusty death. Out, out, brief candle!
	Life's but a walking shadow, a poor player
	That struts and frets his hour upon the stage
	And then is heard no more. It is a tale
	Told by an idiot, full of sound and fury,
	Signifying nothing.

[1] a scream in the dark

[2] mop

[3] probably here a howl or disturbing noise of some sort

[4] drunk

Introduction

All writing can be creatively done, whether it be stories, poems or plays or any of the wide variety of forms that non-fiction takes. This unit will help you to be creative in all of your writing, whatever the task.

It is true that some people seem to have a gift for writing clearly or entertainingly. It is also true, however, that everyone can improve their writing and that good writers work hard at their writing. Whatever you feel is your level of ability, a higher level of writing will help you in many areas of life (not just passing exams).

One of the most obvious starting points is *words*. No matter how good your spelling and punctuation or how neat your handwriting, without carefully chosen words you cannot communicate well. So you need to acquire a good stock of words from which you can choose. You could do that by reading a dictionary or a thesaurus – but that's not much fun. Reading widely, looking up words you don't know as well as working out their meaning from the context – this is the way to widen and deepen your stock of words: your personal reservoir of vocabulary.

You already know thousands of words and you need to make the best use of them. Good writing comes from making decisions about which words are best suited to your purpose. And like most things, practice (and a willingness to experiment) will help enormously.

The first text in this unit is part of a play script, the next three are extracts from works of non-fiction followed by three passages of fiction. The final texts are three poems. There are linking themes within the examples of prose and poetry (violence in the one, love and loss in the other). More importantly, all the texts are examples of carefully crafted writing and all have features from which you can learn.

TEXT 1

This play by Robert Bolt is a comedy set in the legendary time when knights went off to do brave deeds, such as slaying dragons and rescuing maidens. In the opening scene, the writer introduces some of the main characters and sets the plot in motion.

- What kinds of character would you expect to find in a tale of knights of old?
- What does the title suggest to you about the kind of play it is?

The Thwarting of BARON BOLLIGREW

(At a round table sit the **Duke** and the **Knights** … The seat on **Duke**'s L is vacant, and other empty ones are to be seen round the table.)

Storyteller Sir Digby Vayne-Trumpington!
Trumpington enters.

Duke Ah, there you are, Trumpington. Glad to have you back. Got the tip of the dragon's tail?
Trumpington places the bright blue tail-tip on the table. The Duke inspects it.
Not very big, is it?

Trumpington It was not a large dragon, Your Grace, no; but singularly vicious.

First Knight They can be tricky, those little blue beggars.
There is a murmur of agreement.

Duke Not complaining, Trumpington. We can't all be St Georges, can we?
While Trumpington sits, there is a fanfare.

Storyteller Sir Graceless Strongbody!
There is a pause, all looking off expectantly.

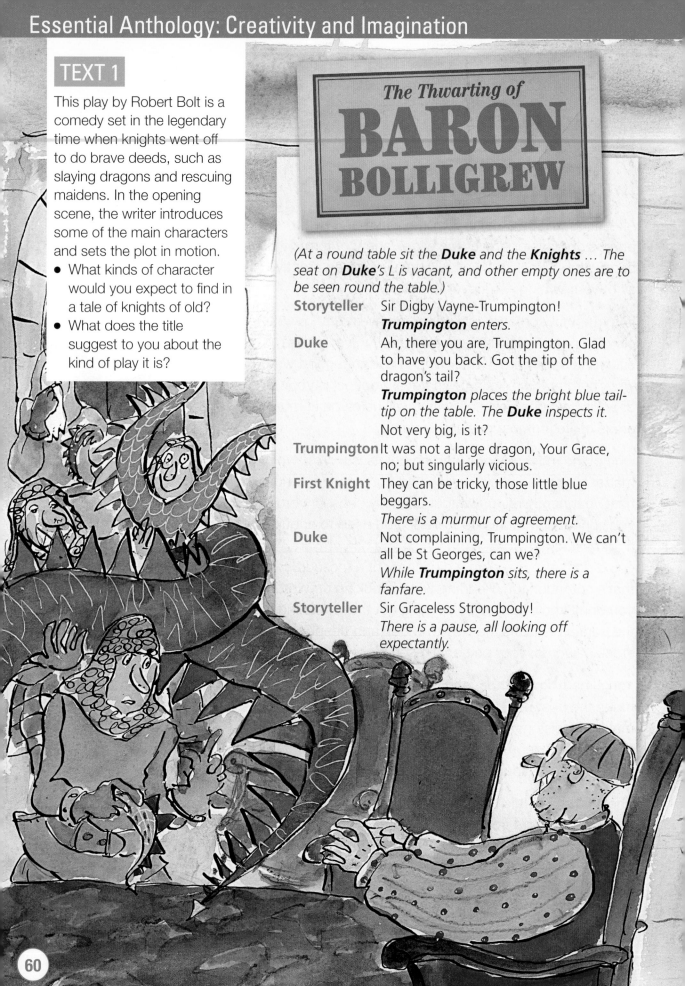

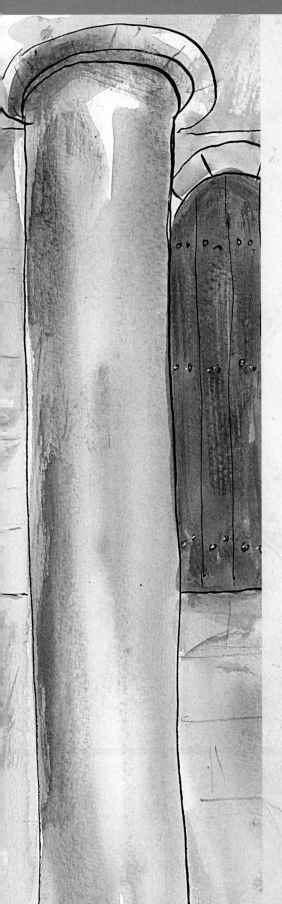

Duke	(*Indulgently.*)[1] Likes to make an entrance, Strongbody … (*The pause continues. Less indulgently.*) Call him again.
Storyteller	Sir Grace …!
	Strongbody *enters dragging a huge green tail. Murmurs of appreciation and then polite clapping come from the* **Knights**.
Duke	I must *say*, Graceless! I think we'll have this stuffed, gentlemen. How d'you do it?
Strongbody	(*Gruffly.*) Oh, usual methods, ye know.
Duke	Aha – "Deeds not Words", the old Strongbody motto.
	There is another fanfare.
Storyteller	Sir Percival Smoothely-Smoothe!
	Smoothe *enters.*
Duke	Good show, Smoothe; back on time as usual. Find your dragon?
	Smoothe *puts down two red tail-tips.*
	Good Lord, *two* dragons!
Smoothe	No, Your Grace, one dragon with two tails.
Duke	Well I never saw such a thing in my life. Gave you a bit of trouble I dare say?
Smoothe	(*Sitting.*) Not really, Your Grace. It seemed to be confused.
Duke	Ah, modest, modest. I like that, Smoothe, like it. Well now, who's missing? (*Looking at the vacant seat to his L.*) Oh, Oblong. Not like him to be late. Well we'll just wait for Oblong, gentlemen, and then I have a little announcement to make, yes …
	There is another fanfare.
Storyteller	Sir Oblong fitz Oblong!
	Sir Oblong fitz Oblong *enters sadly.*
Duke	There you are, Oblong; mission accomplished?
Oblong	Yes, Your Grace.
Duke	Got the tail?
Oblong	Yes, Your Grace.
Duke	(*Kindly.*) Well perk up, man. Whatever's the matter?
Oblong	(*Producing a tail.*) It was a very small dragon, Your Grace. Small and, er, pink. I don't think it can have been fully grown. It meant no harm I'm sure. (*He regards the small pink tail on the table, then takes a handkerchief from the sleeve of his armour and blows his nose.*)

[1] tolerantly

Duke	Now Oblong, we all know how you feel about animals, and I'm sure respect you for it. (*He looks round.*) *There is a murmur of confirmation from the* **Knights***. But* – Duty First – eh?
Oblong	(*Bracing.*) Yes, Your Grace. (*He sits L of* **Duke***.*)
Duke	That's it. (*Patting* **Oblong***'s shoulder as he sits.*) Never knew an Oblong hold back in the face of duty. (*Briskly.*) Now, Juniper my dear chap, read the next item on the agenda will you?
Juniper	Er, "Activities for the coming Season", Your Grace.
Duke	Exactly! (*Rising.*) Gentlemen, a happy announcement: There *are* no activities for the coming season. These (*The tails on the table.*) were the last dragons in the Dukedom. Thanks to your untiring efforts over the years our peasantry may now reap their harvests – and pay their taxes – without interference. Our townsfolk can make their profits – and pay their taxes freely. And in short, there isn't a blessed thing for us to do. *The* **Knights** *rise and congratulate one another noisily shaking hands, patting backs, etc. The hubbub dies and they all sit.*
Oblong	How perfectly splendid, Your Grace.
Duke	Isn't it, isn't it?
Oblong	Now we can move on somewhere else.
Duke	(*Faintly.*) Er, "move on", Oblong?
Oblong	Yes, Your Grace.
Duke	Whatever for?
Oblong	(*Mildly puzzled.*) To succour[2] the poor and needy, Your Grace. Up North, for instance – dragons, barons, goblins. Having a very thin time of it up North, the poor and needy.
Duke	But my dear fellow – the climate!
Oblong	Well, South, then, Your Grace.
Smoothe	(*Gently.*) May I say something, Your Grace?
Duke	Smoothe! Yes! Please, please.
Smoothe	Well gentlemen, we've put this district into some sort of shape – and it's not been easy as you know. It seems to me we've earned a breather.
Duke	Earned a breather. Well said, Smoothe. Late lie-in in the morning. Bit of jousting in the afternoon perhaps. Substantial supper; jolly good game of musical bumps and off to bed. (*Appealing all round.*) Where's the harm in that? *A murmur of considered agreement.* I'll put it to the vote. Democratic procedure – Can't say fairer than that, Oblong. All those in favour – of the programme just outlined, please say "Aye".
All but Oblong	Aye!
Duke	Thank you. All those in favour of moving on, to wild, wet, baron and dragon infested areas, please say "Aye".
Oblong	Er, Aye.
Duke	(*Cheerfully.*) Well there it is, old man. You're outvoted.
Oblong	(*Diffident*).[3] Under the terms of our Charter, Your Grace, I *think* a vote on this subject has to be unanimous. Nobody must disagree.

2 help, comfort
3 shy, hesitant

This text is from *Skimming Stones and other ways of being in the wild* by Rob Cowen and Leo Critchley. It is partly an autobiographical account of outdoor experiences and partly an instruction guide on how to do and make things in the wild, such as damming a stream and foraging for food. The writers are not tough outdoor guys; they just like doing things outdoors.

- Do these activities only apply to males?
- The book contains diagrams; where would they be most appropriate in this extract?

BUILD A DEN

Turning fallen wood and loose leaves into a home from home, a place that will keep you warm and dry overnight, needn't require chainsaw or axe. In fact, a basic debris den can be made quickly in almost any woodland with nothing but your bare hands.

The first thing to do is to choose a good spot. Somewhere with lots of leaf litter and dead wood makes the job easiest. The important thing is to find a clear area that is at least twice as big as the proposed shelter, which will be roughly one and a half times your body length when lying down. Lie on the ground and try the space out for size and comfort, avoiding any roots or patches of uneven earth. Look up and take notice of what is above you. Falling branches can be a serious hazard, especially in windy conditions. Beech trees have been known to suddenly drop a sizeable branch in dry weather to save water, and while a stately oak tree is less likely to shed its appendages, you should stay on the safe side. Avoid setting up camp too close to the trunk of any large tree.

Next, start collecting your key pieces: two sticks about the same size, a metre in length and around 7 to 10 centimetres in diameter that both fork into a 'Y'-shaped end. These will create your entrance and bear most of the weight so choose strong, sturdy branches that fit together well. Prop them against one another, using the divisions at the end to interlink them before looking for the third piece of the frame: a long spine to sit on top that will create a triangular pyramid. This will dictate the size of the internal area so it needs to be longer than you. Lay it across both the interlocked 'Y' shapes and test the whole thing for stability. If it feels secure, check you can get your whole body inside, including a 30-centimetre gap from your head to the entrance as changing it later will undo much of the work. Is there enough room for your feet to stick straight up towards the tapered end? Can you get yourself in through the triangular entrance easily? Remember, a den perfectly tailored to its occupant is best, so if you're making a child-sized shelter, start with a smaller initial frame.

To cover it, first collect lots of sticks ranging from a metre down to about 10 centimetres in length. Place the longest at the entrance and work your way along the spine, covering each side. Site them a few centimetres apart and point the tops slightly forward towards the entrance. Make sure the sticks are close enough together so a leaf litter covering won't fall through and that they project no more than a few centimetres over the spine. Those that do will provide a pathway for rain to trickle in. Once these 'ribs' are in place, lay smaller twigs on top. Don't be too fussy, but loosely hook and weave any little kinks and spindly side branches in between to create a rough lattice.

When the den has an equal covering all around, start burying it in great bundles of leaf litter. Pile armfuls on the sides of the frame, building up from the bottom and over the spine in layers until the whole thing is covered by debris to at least a depth of 40 centimetres. It may take a little time, but this thick layer will provide insulation and waterproofing as effectively as anything manmade. Finally, lay some light, dead branches over the top to hold the covering in place. If trying to save time or short on leaves, a tarpaulin will cover just as well, but you lose the pleasure of creating a den that blends back into the woodland. Why cut yourself off from nature with a layer of plastic? Better to put the tarpaulin down on the inside. Body heat is lost through contact with the cold ground, so when sleeping in a den, it is a good idea to use a foam mat as well as a sleeping bag.

As soon as we entered the Cornish wood, we felt less exposed to the April air. There is almost a sense of being inside when among the trees or, at least, some other half-way state between indoors and outdoors. From the fields beyond, it was an impenetrable green mass, but stepping through the bordering thickets of holly and hawthorn suddenly there was concealed space. Rooms stretched beyond rooms, each a separate shape and design. It was like a natural Tardis, or pushing through the fur coats of the wardrobe into C.S. Lewis's Narnia. The leaves muffled much of the sound of the lively spring wind, and there was a sense of still closeness very different from being in the open fields beyond. We felt almost as though we'd walked in on the beech, sycamore and oak in intense conversation, our footsteps hushing them into whispers.

Falling silent for a moment, the sense of reverence was akin to that which preacher Henry Ward Beecher noted, 'Of all men's works of art, a cathedral is the greatest. A vast and majestic tree is greater than that.' Monuments surrounded us, but with none of the impersonal coldness of some places of worship. The high ceiling of the canopy was church-like, vaulted and flooded with diffused[1] light; natural stained glass in the bright sunshine. Beneath, the ground was softly carpeted with leaves. A nearby stump provided a stool, a fallen trunk a bench. This was a spot as old as England and, like stumbling upon a mystical hollow down a forgotten track, we were entranced.

---

[1] dispersed, gentle

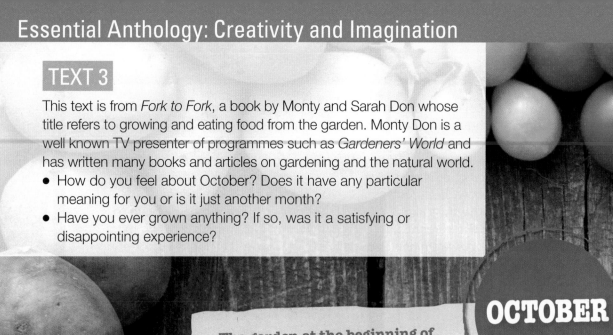

TEXT 3

This text is from *Fork to Fork*, a book by Monty and Sarah Don whose title refers to growing and eating food from the garden. Monty Don is a well known TV presenter of programmes such as *Gardeners' World* and has written many books and articles on gardening and the natural world.

- How do you feel about October? Does it have any particular meaning for you or is it just another month?
- Have you ever grown anything? If so, was it a satisfying or disappointing experience?

OCTOBER

The garden at the beginning of October flatters to deceive. The sun still has the heat to warm through your shirt, still carries the tang of summer during the middle of the day. But no one is fooled. This is not the real thing but borrowed from summer, little more than a good memory. Autumn has arrived. The leaves are changing colour daily and the air has an almost tangible opacity[1] you only find in autumn.

Because this is borrowed time, because the frosts will come any day, these days are as precious as jewels. It is too dark and cold to eat out in the evening but there are still meals in the garden in the middle of the day. At its best, October sun and October light before the first frost are as beautiful as any other time in the garden. At the start of the month the flower borders still have their glowing richness that the frost will steal and are filled with russets and crimsons, purples and oranges, and the grass has an emerald intensity that is lost in the dry days of summer.

In the vegetable garden the last of the summer vegetables overlap winter ones like the leeks and cabbages that are now maturing fast. Tomatoes, sweet corn, Florence fennel, squashes and pumpkins ripen as a race against failing heat and light and, inevitably, all have to be collected in a spirit of compromise between saving what is good and accepting that some will not ripen at all.

[…]

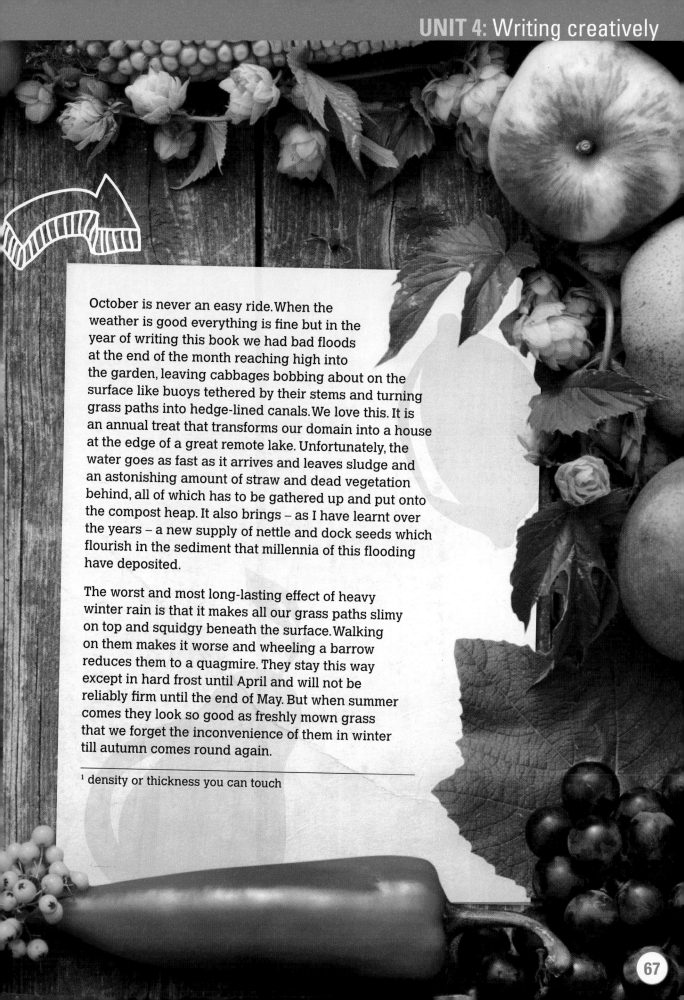

October is never an easy ride. When the weather is good everything is fine but in the year of writing this book we had bad floods at the end of the month reaching high into the garden, leaving cabbages bobbing about on the surface like buoys tethered by their stems and turning grass paths into hedge-lined canals. We love this. It is an annual treat that transforms our domain into a house at the edge of a great remote lake. Unfortunately, the water goes as fast as it arrives and leaves sludge and an astonishing amount of straw and dead vegetation behind, all of which has to be gathered up and put onto the compost heap. It also brings – as I have learnt over the years – a new supply of nettle and dock seeds which flourish in the sediment that millennia of this flooding have deposited.

The worst and most long-lasting effect of heavy winter rain is that it makes all our grass paths slimy on top and squidgy beneath the surface. Walking on them makes it worse and wheeling a barrow reduces them to a quagmire. They stay this way except in hard frost until April and will not be reliably firm until the end of May. But when summer comes they look so good as freshly mown grass that we forget the inconvenience of them in winter till autumn comes round again.

---

[1] density or thickness you can touch

In *A Taste of India*, Madhur Jaffrey divides the book into chapters according to regions of India, such as Kerala. She spends the first part of each chapter describing the area before moving on to the food and then to particular recipes.

- How much do you know about different foods from the various parts of India?
- Where is Kerala? Can you find it on a map?

KERALA

Heaven must be a bit like Kerala, an ancient strip of lush, tropical land that slithers sensuously[1] down the coast of south-western India. Devout Hindus, Muslims, Christians and Jews live in harmony here, the steeples and spires of their age-old temples, mosques, churches and synagogues all aspiring to some common goodness, side by side.

Blessed not only with the winds of tolerance but with temperatures that hover around the constantly balmy mark and plentiful rain, the land in Kerala produces with the enthusiasm of a pampered hothouse.

[…]

The gardens, then as now, are kitchen gardens which do not sit neatly and demurely[2] on one side of the house as a European herb garden might, but encircle it with some abandon. Houses often disappear entirely within their verdant, forest-like foliage. Black pepper vines clamber tenaciously[3] up mango trees, the peppercorns huddling together in bright green clusters like bunches of embryo[4] grapes. Nutmeg fruit hang like tennis balls, ready to split open and offer both their nuts and their special bonus, curls of tangerine-coloured mace. Cinnamon, clove and tamarind trees compete for a view of the sky while cardamom stays close to the ground, hugging its mother bush. There are ginger and turmeric plants as well, sending fingers [of their tubers] into the cool dark earth. Above all, there are the two trees that give the foods of Kerala their special character – the sweetly aromatic curry leaf tree … and the arching, swaying coconut palm.

---

[1] richly, luxuriously

[2] modestly or shyly

[3] stubbornly

[4] tiny starting point

TEXT 5

This text is from F.E. Higgins' novel *The Lunatic's Curse*, set in an imaginary and rather unpleasant world that seems to have the technology of a rural country in the 19th century. In this text, the hero's father, Ambrose, is imprisoned in a dungeon with the always optimistic Hooper.

- Which gives us more information in this text, conversation or thoughts?
- Is Hooper a believable character?

THE GREAT ESCAPE PLAN

Ambrose Oswald Grammaticus turned over slowly in his incredibly uncomfortable bed – if a pile of straw on the rocky floor of a cell not big enough to jump in could be called a bed. He groaned as his bones creaked. On the wall beside him was a tally, sets of four parallel lines crossed with a diagonal; over a hundred days crossed off.

'Here, Ambrose, have a bit of this,' said a voice close to him. 'You've got to eat, for when we get out, you'll need energy.'

'Get out?' Ambrose managed a laugh. 'Tell me, Hooper, how are we to do that? Are we not locked in all day and all night?' He looked over at the cell door. Yes, as he expected, the rusty iron-barred door was firmly closed as ever.

'Don't be like that,' said the cheerful voice.

Ambrose had grown used to his companion's unrelentingly sunny nature, but he still marvelled at the fellow's ability to see the silver lining not just on some clouds, but on *every* cloud, no matter how black it might be. If it had been a century or so later the fellow would have been diagnosed with Felix Semper syndrome,[1] a disease characterized by the sufferer being in a permanent state of happiness, gullible and trusting to the extreme, and completely incapable of relating to the real world. But, ironically enough, being permanently happy, Hooper was able to take his imprisonment in his stride.

'And is that really such a bad thing?' Ambrose often asked himself as he watched Hooper smiling day and night (not that he could tell the difference between the two in here). He could not deny that this blithe fellow had kept him from giving up

for a long time. But these last few days he had felt a change. He was ill. His whole body ached, his head throbbed and he was growing weaker, racked with terrible cravings. He felt as if he had reached the end of his powers of endurance. He looked at Hooper. He was hardly any better off, not a pick of meat on his bones. He laughed to himself. They truly were a revolting pair.

'Ah, don't be like that, Ambrose,' cajoled Hooper softly. 'Never say never! Eh? What would young Rex think if he knew that his father was about to give up?'

At the mention of his son's name Ambrose made an effort and sat up. Hooper, a short, red-elbowed man with bushy eyebrows, was proffering a bowl of what could only be described as mud soup.

'What's in it?' he asked.

'Who knows?' laughed Hooper. 'No meat, I'll wager, but it don't taste that bad.'

Meat! The very thought of it caused Ambrose to quiver violently. He cradled the bowl awkwardly with his left arm and took a spoonful, and resisted the urge to spit it out. Then he took another. Revolting as it was, his starved body craved nourishment and he ate without stopping. A mouse crept out from the corner and looked at him but he kicked it away. Hooper grabbed it. 'Something for later,' he said, and broke its neck.

---

[1] disorder, illness

This text is from *Jamaica Inn*, a novel by Daphne du Maurier set in the early 19th century in the wild moors of Cornwall. Following the death of her mother, Mary has been sent to live with her uncle Joss and his wife. She learns that her uncle is the ringleader of a gang of criminals involved in smuggling and worse …

- How do we know immediately that Mary is not in the room?
- Where does the writer use senses other than hearing?

AN INCIDENT …
A MURDER?

Mary heard the scraping of a chair, and the man rise to his feet, but at the same time someone thumped his fist on the table and swore, and her uncle lifted his voice for the first time.

'Not so fast, my friend,' he said, 'not so fast. You're soaked in this business up to your neck, and be damned to your blasted conscience! I tell you there's no going back on it now; it's too late; too late for you and for all of us. I've been doubtful of you from the first, with your gentleman's airs and your clean cuffs, and by God I've proved myself right. Harry, bolt the door over there and put the bar across it.'

There was a sudden scuffle and a cry, and the sound of someone falling, and at the same time the table crashed to the floor, and the door to the yard was slammed. Once more the pedlar laughed, odious and obscene, and he began to whistle one of his songs. 'Shall we tickle him up like Silly Sam?' he said, breaking off in the middle. 'He'd be a little body without his fine clothes. I could do with his watch and chain, too; poor men of the road like myself haven't the money to go buying watches. Tickle him up with the whip, Joss, and let's see the colour of his skin.'

'Shut your mouth, Harry, and do as you're told,' answered the landlord. 'Stand where you are by the door and prick him with your knife if he tries to pass you. Now, look here, Mr lawyer-clerk, or whatever you are in Truro town, you've made a fool of yourself tonight, but you're not going to make a fool of me. You'd like to walk out of that door, wouldn't you, and get on your horse, and be away to Bodmin? Yes, and by nine in the morning you'd have every magistrate in the country at Jamaica Inn, and a regiment of soldiers into the bargain. That's your fine idea, isn't it?'

Mary could hear the stranger breathe heavily, and he must have been hurt in the scuffle, for when his voice came it was jerky and contracted, as though he were in pain. 'Do your devil's work if you must,' he muttered. 'I can't stop you, and I give you my word I'll not inform against you. But join you I will not, and there's my last word to you both.'

There was a silence, and then Joss Merlyn spoke again. 'Have a care,' he said softly. 'I heard another man say that once, and five minutes later he was treading the air. On the end of a rope it was, my friend, and his big toe missed the floor by half an inch. I asked him if he liked to be so near the ground, but he didn't answer. The rope forced the tongue out of his mouth, and he bit it clean in half. They said afterwards he had taken seven and three-quarter minutes to die.'

Outside in the passage Mary felt her neck and her forehead go clammy with sweat, and her arms and legs were weighted suddenly, as though with lead. Little black specks flickered before her eyes, and with a growing sense of horror she realised that she was probably going to faint.

She had one thought in her mind, and that was to grope her way back to the deserted hall and reach the shadow of the clock; whatever happened she must not fall here and be discovered. Mary backed away from the beam of light, and felt along the wall with her hands. Her knees were shaking now and she knew that at any moment they would give beneath her. Already a surge of sickness rose inside her, and her head was swimming.

Her uncle's voice came from very far away, as though he spoke with his hands against his mouth. 'Leave me alone with him, Harry,' he said; 'there'll be no more work for you tonight at Jamaica. Take his horse and be off, and cast him loose the other side of Camelford. I'll settle this business by myself.'

Somehow Mary found her way to the hall, and, hardly conscious of what she was doing, she turned the handle of the parlour door and stumbled inside. Then she crumpled in a heap on the floor, her head between her knees.

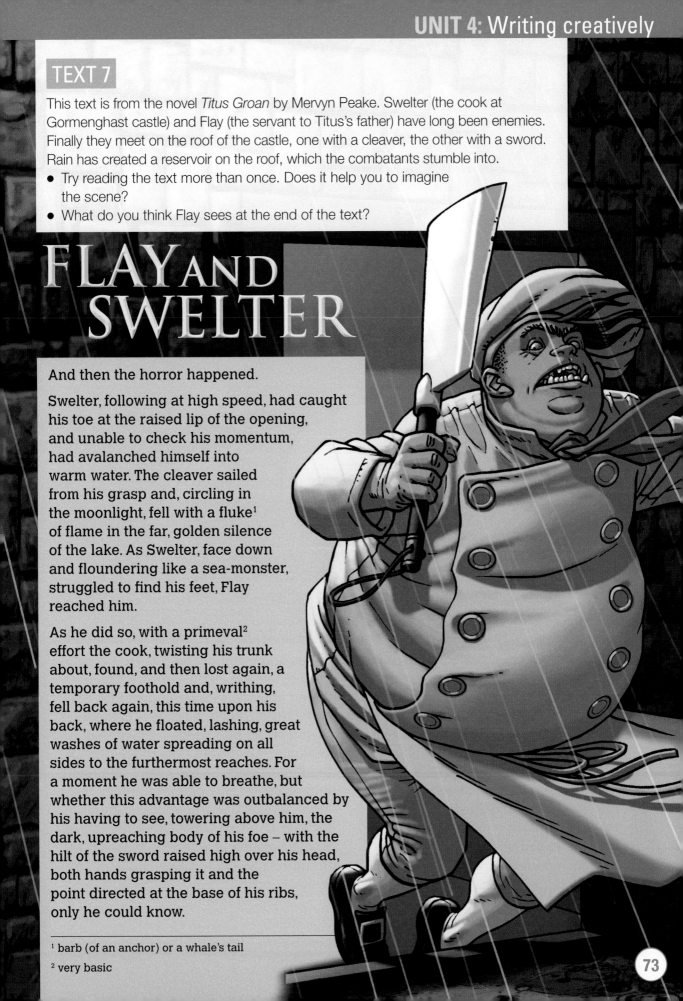

TEXT 7

This text is from the novel *Titus Groan* by Mervyn Peake. Swelter (the cook at Gormenghast castle) and Flay (the servant to Titus's father) have long been enemies. Finally they meet on the roof of the castle, one with a cleaver, the other with a sword. Rain has created a reservoir on the roof, which the combatants stumble into.

- Try reading the text more than once. Does it help you to imagine the scene?
- What do you think Flay sees at the end of the text?

FLAY AND SWELTER

And then the horror happened.

Swelter, following at high speed, had caught his toe at the raised lip of the opening, and unable to check his momentum, had avalanched himself into warm water. The cleaver sailed from his grasp and, circling in the moonlight, fell with a fluke[1] of flame in the far, golden silence of the lake. As Swelter, face down and floundering like a sea-monster, struggled to find his feet, Flay reached him.

As he did so, with a primeval[2] effort the cook, twisting his trunk about, found, and then lost again, a temporary foothold and, writhing, fell back again, this time upon his back, where he floated, lashing, great washes of water spreading on all sides to the furthermost reaches. For a moment he was able to breathe, but whether this advantage was outbalanced by his having to see, towering above him, the dark, upreaching body of his foe – with the hilt of the sword raised high over his head, both hands grasping it and the point directed at the base of his ribs, only he could know.

[1] barb (of an anchor) or a whale's tail

[2] very basic

The water about him was reddening and his eyes, like marbles of gristle, rolled in the moonlight as the sword plunged steeply. Flay did not trouble to withdraw it. It remained like a mast of steel whose sails had fallen to the decks where, as though with a life of their own, unconnected with wind or tide, they leapt and shook in ghastly turbulence. At the mast-head, the circular sword hilt, like a crow's nest, boasted no inch-high pirate.

Flay, leaning against the outer wall of the Hall of Spiders, the water up to his knees and watching with his eyes half-closed, the last death throes, heard a sound above him and in a shudder of gooseflesh turned his eyes and found them staring into a face – a face that smiled in silver light from the depths of the Hall beyond. Its eyes were circular and its mouth was opening, and as the lunar silence came down as though for ever in a vast white sheet, the long-drawn screech of a death owl tore it, as though it had been calico,[3] from end to end.

---

[3] thin cloth

TEXT 8

At the time of writing, Carol Ann Duffy is Poet Laureate. Her poem 'Valentine' deliberately offers something completely unexpected and, in the context, strange.

- An onion can be interpreted in a number of ways. What do you think the poem says about the person offering it and the person receiving it?
- How would you feel if you were given an onion when you were expecting a more traditional gift?

Not a red rose or a satin heart.

I give you an onion.
It is a moon wrapped in brown paper.
It promises light
like the careful undressing of love.

Here.
It will blind you with tears
like a lover.
It will make your reflection
a wobbling photo of grief.

I am trying to be truthful.

Not a cute card or a kissogram.

I give you an onion.
Its fierce kiss will stay on your lips,
possessive and faithful
as we are,
for as long as we are.

Take it.
Its platinum loops shrink to a wedding-ring,
if you like.
Lethal.
Its scent will cling to your fingers,
cling to your knife.

TEXT 9

Edna St Vincent Millay was a prolific and popular American writer during the first half of the 20th century.
In this poem, she rejects the advice that time will bring relief.
Everywhere reminds her of the departed (or dead) love and even places where there is no shared memory cause her to experience the same feeling of loss.

- People often say 'Time will heal'. Is it true?
- What form does this poem take?

TIME DOES NOT BRING RELIEF; YOU ALL HAVE LIED

Time does not bring relief; you all have lied

Who told me time would ease me of my pain!

I miss him in the weeping of the rain;

I want him at the shrinking of the tide;

The old snows melt from every mountain-side,

And last year's leaves are smoke in every lane;

But last year's bitter loving must remain

Heaped on my heart, and my old thoughts abide.[1]

There are a hundred places where I fear

To go,—so with his memory they brim!

And entering with relief some quiet place

Where never fell his foot or shone his face

I say, "There is no memory of him here!"

And so stand stricken,[2] so remembering him!

---

[1] remain
[2] tormented

TEXT 10

D.H. Lawrence was an acclaimed novelist and essayist as well as a poet. 'Piano' is one of his earlier poems; later he wrote less structured 'free verse'. 'Piano' creates a mood of nostalgia as he remembers a particularly pleasant scene from his childhood. The memory is triggered by hearing someone singing, accompanied by a piano.

- Do you have memories that are triggered by sights, sounds or smells?
- 'The great black piano' hints that the writer might be where?

PIANO

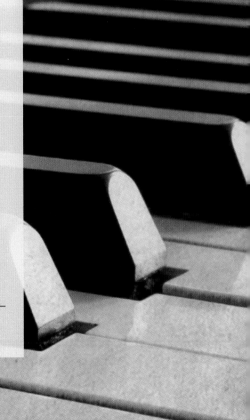

Softly, in the dusk, a woman is singing to me;

Taking me back down the vista of years, till I see

A child sitting under the piano, in the boom of the tingling strings

And pressing the small, poised feet of a mother who smiles as
    she sings.

In spite of myself, the insidious[1] mastery of song

Betrays me back, till the heart of me weeps to belong

To the old Sunday evenings at home, with winter outside

And hymns in the cosy parlour, the tinkling piano our guide.

So now it is vain for the singer to burst into clamour

With the great black piano appassionato.[2] The glamour

Of childish days is upon me, my manhood is cast

Down in the flood of remembrance, I weep like a child for the past.

---

[1] stealthy

[2] loud and with passion

UNIT 5 Exploration

Introduction

We humans have always explored the world. From trying to group and name everything in nature to seeking to map the entire globe, we have demonstrated an almost unquenchable thirst for knowledge and understanding of our environment. At the same time, and almost as strong, has been the drive to share that experience: at first through travel journals and letters home and now online and through the media as well as through the printed word. This desire to share remarkable experiences has given rise to a wealth of material that relates to the theme of exploration.

The texts in this unit celebrate the drives to explore and communicate. They also enable you to study the subject of English in a new way. This is the final unit in the book and it doesn't aim to introduce you to a particular kind of writing, as previous units have done. Instead, it gives you opportunities to practise different skills in English whilst encountering texts which have only one thing in common: their theme.

Through these texts, you will experience language produced for different purposes and audiences, and in various forms. You will also have the opportunity to use language in a range of different ways yourself – all linked to the theme of exploration. There are non-fiction informative texts for a variety of audiences from children to adults, alongside autobiographical extracts, a letter and a transcript from a television programme. Fiction texts include an early science-fiction extract, a passage from a children's novel and a couple of poems. As you might expect, this range of material will ask you to read and think in a variety of ways.

TEXT 1

This text is by the Australian poet,
C.J. Dennis, and was first published
in 1921. Dennis was known
particularly for humorous poems.
This poem is taken from a collection
of poems and stories for children.

- What do you find most interesting
  or enjoyable about this poem?
- What do you think makes a
  journey an exploration rather than
  just a trip?

The **ANT** EXPLORER

Once a little sugar ant made up his mind to roam –
To fare away far away, far away from home.
He had eaten all his breakfast, and he had his Ma's consent
To see what he should chance to see and here's the way he went –
Up and down a fern frond, round and round a stone,
Down a gloomy gully where he loathed to be alone,
Up a mighty mountain range, seven inches high,
Through the fearful forest grass that nearly hid the sky,
Out along a bracken bridge, bending in the moss,
Till he reached a dreadful desert that was feet and feet across.
'Twas a dry, deserted desert, and a trackless land to tread,
He wished that he was home again and tucked-up tight in bed.
His little legs were wobbly, his strength was nearly spent,
And so he turned around again and here's the way he went –
Back away from desert lands feet and feet across,
Back along the bracken bridge bending in the moss,
Through the fearful forest grass shutting out the sky,
Up a mighty mountain range seven inches high,
Down a gloomy gully, where he loathed to be alone,
Up and down a fern frond and round and round a stone.
A dreary ant, a weary ant, resolved no more to roam,
He staggered up the garden path and popped back home.

TEXT 2

This text is from *West of the Moon*, a novel for older children and younger teenagers by Katherine Langrish. It's a fantasy adventure about a Viking community. Here, the main characters – Peer and Hilde – are travelling across the sea in a dragon boat called *Water Snake* to a new country.

- What impression of the journey do you get from this text? What kind of mood has been created?
- What can you tell about the various characters and their relationships from this passage?

WEST *of the* MOON

"There are no trolls in Vinland," said Magnus confidently.

Peer sat with his back against the curve of the side, rocking to the steady up and down of the ship. He could see sky, but not sea, and it was comforting to shut out for a while the sight of all that lonely vastness. The sun had just set: the top half of the sail still caught a ruddy glow on its western side.

Water Snake was on the starboard tack, lifting and diving over the waves in a rhythm as easy as breathing. They were far from land – further than Peer had ever been before. This big ship seemed very small now – a speck of dust under a wide sky.

The day had passed simply. At home there would be a hundred things to do: ploughing fields, chopping firewood, patching boats, mending nets. Here there was only one purpose, to sail on and on into the west.

Like an enormous, slewed curtain, the sail had almost cut off the front of the ship from the rear. To be heard by someone in a different part of the vessel, you had to shout across the wind. Just now, Harald was steering, and Peer was in the bows, almost as far away from him as it was possible to get. He leaned back, watching Loki scramble over the stacks of crates and barrels amidships, sticking his nose in everywhere. Loki was having no problems adjusting to his new life at sea!

And neither was Hilde. On leaving home this morning, she'd been as close to tears as Peer had ever seen her – but now she was sitting on a crossbeam, chatting to some of the men. Trust Hilde, he thought to himself with a rueful smile. She knew the names of half the crew already and was finding out about the others.

"No trolls in Vinland?" she was saying now. "So you've been there, Magnus – you've sailed with Gunnar before?"

"That's right." Magnus was a middle-aged man, his face criss-crossed with tiny lines from screwing up his eyes against sun and weather. He beamed at Hilde. "Me, and Halfdan, and young Floki here, we were all with the skipper on his last voyage. Never saw a troll."

TEXT 3

This text is the introduction to a children's non-fiction book by wildlife TV presenter, Nick Baker. It explains in detail how to capture and care for different species of minibeasts.

- How does this extract relate to the theme of exploration?
- What do you think is the purpose of this text: what does Nick Baker want to happen as a result of this writing?

Welcome to
BUG ZOO!!

Why start a bug zoo? Well, why not? Just because bugs are everywhere doesn't mean that they're any less interesting than the animals you might see in a real zoo. In fact, the chances are that you know more about the exotic animals in a zoo than you do about the tiny creatures living right under your nose.

When I was growing up, my parents wouldn't let me keep animals in the house and I can't say I blame them. It didn't help my cause when my stick insects got out and defoliated my mum's houseplants or when I forgot to put the lid back on my ant city ... But such mishaps didn't hold me back. We had an old shed and I quickly purloined it for my collection. Armed with a curious mind and a few jars, **I built my first bug zoo**, and wow, did it open my eyes!

Each pot, pickle jar and matchbox was a source of wonder, a dramatic little world with as much excitement as any TV soap opera. I saw MURDER and **cannibalism**,[1] slashing blades and chemical warfare. I watched caterpillars being reincarnated as butterflies. And I learnt first-hand that **there's nothing ladylike about a ladybird!**

Starting a bug zoo is the perfect way to immerse yourself in the alien world of bugs. When you get down to their level (and that means getting *really* close – eye to compound eye, finger to feeler), it puts a fresh spin on the way you see things: a lawn becomes an exotic savannah,[2] a hedge becomes a jungle, a garden pond becomes as mysterious as the deep sea. You don't even need to use your imagination – there are unexplored worlds right on your doorstep, and the fantastical animals are real. You just have to open your eyes.

Building a zoo means you can become an explorer, a hunter, a collector of fine zoological specimens and, of course, a zoo keeper. You don't need much to get started – just a table and a few jars will do. And you can capture your exhibits anywhere. Tune into their world and I will promise you this: you will never, ever be bored again.

Happy hunting!

---

[1] eating others of your own species

[2] a grassland habitat

The First Men in the Moon

Those who have only seen the starry sky from the earth cannot imagine its appearance when the vague, half luminous veil of our air has been withdrawn. The stars we see on earth are the mere scattered survivors that penetrate our misty atmosphere. But now at last I could realise the meaning of the hosts of heaven!

Stranger things we were presently to see, but that airless, star-dusted sky! Of all things, I think that will be one of the last I shall forget.

The little window vanished with a click, another beside it snapped open and instantly closed, and then a third, and for a moment I had to close my eyes because of the blinding splendour of the waning moon.

For a space I had to stare at Cavor and the white-lit things about me to season my eyes to light again, before I could turn them towards that pallid glare.

[…]

It was curiously unlike earthly experience, too, to have the light coming up to one. On earth light falls from above, or comes slanting down sideways, but here it came from beneath our feet, and to see our shadows we had to look up.

At first it gave me a sort of vertigo to stand only on thick glass and look down upon the moon through hundreds of thousands of miles of vacant space; but this sickness passed very speedily. And then – the splendour of the sight!

Sea Fever

TEXT 5

This text is one of John Masefield's most famous and popular poems. In 1891, at the age of 13, Masefield joined HMS *Conway* – a training ship to prepare boys to be sailors. He was not happy or successful as a sailor, however, and his first collection of poems was published in 1902.

- What feelings do you think the poet is trying to describe in this poem?
- What explanation does the speaker in the poem give for why he feels as he does?

I must go down to the seas again, to the lonely sea and the sky,

And all I ask is a tall ship and a star to steer her by;

And the wheel's kick and the wind's song and the white sail's shaking,

And a grey mist on the sea's face, and a grey dawn breaking.

I must go down to the seas again, for the call of the running tide

Is a wild call and a clear call that may not be denied;

And all I ask is a windy day with the white clouds flying,

And the flung spray and the blown spume, and the sea-gulls crying.

I must go down to the seas again, to the vagrant gypsy life,

To the gull's way and the whale's way where the wind's like a whetted knife;

And all I ask is a merry yarn from a laughing fellow-rover,

And quiet sleep and a sweet dream when the long trick's over.

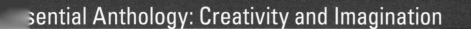

TEXT 6

In this extract from his autobiography, *Looking for Adventure*, Steve Backshall is explaining his thought process when an interviewer asked him 'Why do you do this with your life? What makes you want to continually push yourself? Most people are going to think you're completely insane.'

- How does Backshall convince us that he is 'an anachronism'?
- Have you ever thought about living in another time period? If you had to live in a different time, when would you choose? Why?

Looking for Adventure

I wasn't supposed to be here. I've been dumped out of time. I'm an anachronism,[1] a refugee of circumstance trying to find my place in a shallow, shrink-wrapped modern world.

I know I'm far from alone. Practically every day that passes sees another of my competitors or colleagues paraglide off Everest in a gorilla suit or sail across the Pacific in a bathtub in a desperate search to affirm themselves, and to be the first at something. Anything! A couple of hundred years ago we would perhaps have been real explorers, discovering a world awash with undreamt-of miracles. However, modern explorers are not burly machete-wielding adventurers but big-brained scientists in search of 'the God particle', cold fusion or the cure for cancer. In fact just about everything about the modern world and its silicon chip, silicon chest, fast food, concrete and shining glass exterior leaves me cold, and with a deeply uncomfortable sensation in my belly. Could it be that I'm a savage dumped in modern times like Crocodile Dundee – well, except without the wit, the giant knife or the super-fit American girlfriend? Could this be why I have the niggling sense in the back of my mind that everything around me is somehow wrong?

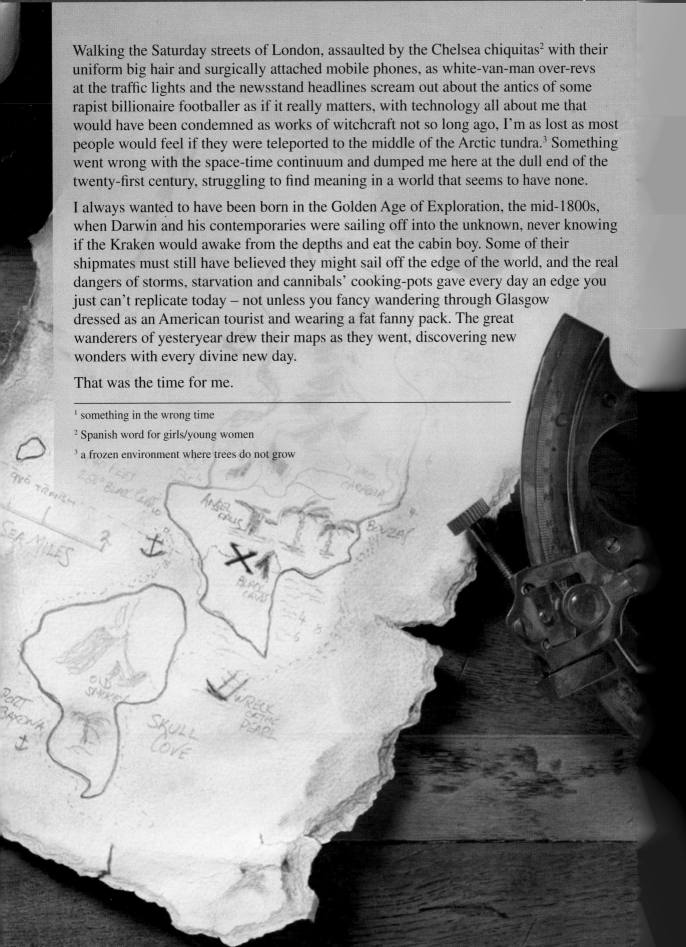

Walking the Saturday streets of London, assaulted by the Chelsea chiquitas[2] with their uniform big hair and surgically attached mobile phones, as white-van-man over-revs at the traffic lights and the newsstand headlines scream out about the antics of some rapist billionaire footballer as if it really matters, with technology all about me that would have been condemned as works of witchcraft not so long ago, I'm as lost as most people would feel if they were teleported to the middle of the Arctic tundra.[3] Something went wrong with the space-time continuum and dumped me here at the dull end of the twenty-first century, struggling to find meaning in a world that seems to have none.

I always wanted to have been born in the Golden Age of Exploration, the mid-1800s, when Darwin and his contemporaries were sailing off into the unknown, never knowing if the Kraken would awake from the depths and eat the cabin boy. Some of their shipmates must still have believed they might sail off the edge of the world, and the real dangers of storms, starvation and cannibals' cooking-pots gave every day an edge you just can't replicate today – not unless you fancy wandering through Glasgow dressed as an American tourist and wearing a fat fanny pack. The great wanderers of yesteryear drew their maps as they went, discovering new wonders with every divine new day.

That was the time for me.

---

[1] something in the wrong time

[2] Spanish word for girls/young women

[3] a frozen environment where trees do not grow

TEXT 7

This extract is adapted from the prologue to Bear Grylls' autobiography, *Mud, Sweat and Tears*. Grylls is well known for his television programmes about survival in difficult environments, and he is also a patron of the Boy Scouts.

- How is the style of this text different from Text 6, which is also from an autobiography?
- What other kinds of text does it remind you of?

MUD SWEAT AND TEARS

The air temperature is minus twenty degrees. I wiggle my fingers but they're still freezing cold. Old frost-nip injuries never let you forget. I blame Everest for that.

'You set?' cameraman Simon asks me, smiling. His rig is prepped and ready.

I smile back. I am unusually nervous. Something doesn't feel quite right.

But I don't listen to the inner voice.

The crisp Northern Canadian Rockies look spectacular this morning. Beneath me is three hundred feet of steep snow and ice. Steep but manageable.

I have done this sort of fast descent many, many times. Never be complacent, the voice says. The voice is always right.

A last deep breath. A look to Simon. We have cut a vital corner. I know it. But I do nothing.

I leap.

I am instantly taken by the speed. Normally I love it. This time I am worried.

I never feel worried in the moment. I know something is wrong.

I am soon travelling at over 40 m.p.h. Feet first down the mountain. The ice races past only inches from my head. This is my world.

I gain even more speed. The edge of the peak gets closer. Time to arrest the fall. I flip nimbly onto my front and drive the ice axe into the snow. A cloud of white spray and ice soars into the air. I can feel the rapid deceleration as I grind the axe deep into the mountain with all my power.

It works like it always does. Like clockwork. Total confidence. One of those rare moments of lucidity.

It is fleeting. Then it is gone.

I am now static. The world hangs still.

Then – bang. Simon, his heavy wooden sledge, plus solid metal camera housing, piles straight into my left thigh. He is doing in excess of 45 m.p.h. There is an instant explosion of pain and noise and white.

It is like a freight train. And I am thrown down the mountain like a doll.

Life stands still. I feel and see it all in slow motion.

Yet in that split-second I have only one realisation: a one-degree different course and the sledge's collision would have been with my head. Without doubt, it would have been my last living thought.

Instead, I am in agony, writhing.

I am crying. They are tears of relief.

I am injured, but I am alive.

I see a helicopter, but hear no sound. Then the hospital. I have been in a few since *Man vs. Wild/Born Survivor: Bear Grylls* began. I hate them.

Countless close shaves.

They all blur. All bad.

Yet all good. I am alive. Life is about the living. I am smiling.

The next day, I forget the crash. To me, it is past. Accidents happen, it was no one's fault.

Lessons learned.

Listen to the voice.

TEXT 8

In October 2012, Felix Baumgartner broke several records by skydiving from 23 miles above the Earth. This newspaper article, published two months later, presents Baumgartner's thoughts and feelings about his jump.

- What dreams for the future do you have? What would you do then if you achieved them?
- What is your opinion about this kind of activity? Do you admire Baumgartner or think he's foolish?

Felix Baumgartner on
Falling from Space

How many people have had the opportunity to see the curvature of the Earth below and a completely black sky above? Sitting at the edge of the craft, preparing to jump, was an unforgettable experience: spectacular, and humbling. Before I jumped I said, "I'm going home now," and that's what I was thinking – with my jump I'd be going home to the people I love. I was also aware I only had 10 minutes of oxygen, so part of me was thinking, "Don't waste too much time. Get going."

As I fell, I was focused on what I needed to do. There was a time when I was spinning that I thought I might be in trouble. But even then I could be calm as I had trained so hard and because we had taken precautions, including a small stabilisation parachute. That would have created drag and slowed me down, so I'm glad I fought to get control and didn't need it. I became the first person to break the speed of sound in freefall.

I trained for five years for the jump – mentally and physically, including things like gripping as it's very hard to use your hands in those gloves. I also learned about all the technical and medical issues involved in a jump from the stratosphere: that was essential to earn the respect of the scientists and doctors on the team and collaborate with them. As a professional base jumper, I was accustomed to being independent.

I always knew death or injury were possible, but I didn't think I would die. I am a very meticulous planner: I look at all the risks, and if they are too high I won't undertake the project. The best thing to result from the jump is still to come. Not only have we proven that a human can successfully break the speed of sound in freefall – which in itself can lead to advancements in emergency bailout – but it's clear from the response we've received that this mission has sparked people to follow their own dreams, whatever they are.

Would I do it again? No. Once I've accomplished something, I'm always ready to move on to the next challenge.

TEXT 9

This transcript is taken from the first episode of the TV series, *Long Way Round*, which showed Ewan McGregor and Charley Boorman riding from London via Europe and Asia to New York on motorbikes.

- What do you think about these plans? Do you think if more people could afford to make trips like this, they would?
- If you could travel anywhere in the world, where would you go? How would you travel?
- How do you react to the idea that there are still places in the world which aren't fully mapped?

Long Way Round

Charley: (Visuals show a map of the journey.) We're gonna ride **twenty** thousand miles and travel through **thirteen** countries.

Ewan: And then we **could** just directly go East through Russia, but we wanna see Kazakhstan and Mongolia (pause) and then ride the **Road** of Bones in far eastern Russia to to Magadan.

Charley: An we're gonna fly to Alaska an go through **Ca**nada, America and New York.

Ewan: This is longer than any bike ride I've ever done, y'know? (Visuals change to close up on Ewan.) This isn't just going out for a ride on my, 'I'm just going out for a ride on my bike!', this is a bit more than that, y'know.

(Scene change – outside in the city, moving, heading towards office buildings.)

Now we've got the route, what we need to do is, is speak to people who **know** a lot about the countries we're gonna pass through.

(Close up on sign outside Kazakhstan Embassy.)

Key:	
(...)	non-verbal details
bold	emphasis
[...]	simultaneous speech
–	speaker follows immediately on

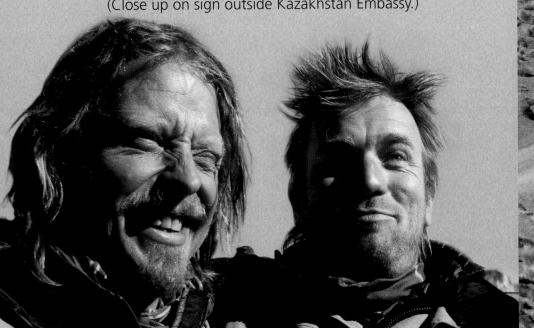

(Scene of Charley and Ewan flicking through books on a shelf, inside Kazakhstan Embassy; Charley fumbles and drops his book; both laugh.)

Charley: I'm sorry. How embarrassing!

Ambassador: Kazakhstan, er, just started developing, er, the capacity to produce maps [Ewan: mm-hmm] and for a **huge** country, you can understand that it is a–

Charley: –an enormous task.

Ewan: Yeah, yeah.

Ambassador: It's a challenging task, therefore–

Ewan: –if we can help, on the way, we can draw some maps.

Ambassador: That will be (laughs)

Ewan: very helpful (laughs).

Ambassador: But I will try to.

Ewan: If we know where we're going– [Ambassador: yes]

Charley: –just a rough idea– [Ambassador: yes]

Ewan: –we can ask people an, y'know, I'm sure we'll be.

Cameraman: East.

Charley: East.

Cameraman: Which way's East?

Ewan: We're going East.

Charley: (Scene shifts to Long Way Round offices.) It's very important for us to learn about the different rituals and customs in each of these countries, like in Mongolia, er, when we're driving our motorbikes, how do you say 'no' to vodka politely?

Advisor: You don't have to drink any, you just kind of take it with your right hand (mimes), maybe put it to your lips, then you give it back to the same person.

Ewan: You don't have to try and spill it [when they're not looking, like that.]

Advisor: [no, you don't have to do that.] No that's fine. They might offer you snuff. It's all the **etiquette**, it's all because they want to give, but sometimes it might actually be an empty snuff bottle, so in effect, um–

Charley: –you just pretend.

Advisor: You pretend (mimes) [to take it an if]

Ewan: [But if there **is**] snuff.

Advisor: If there is snuff, yeah.

Ewan: You can take a little pinch of snuff.

Advisor: There's a whole sort of way, rigmarole of [which hand you take it in.]

Ewan: [Gets round the fact that] we're both giving up smoking by the time we go.

TEXT 10

Gertrude Bell was an English traveller, writer and explorer who worked for the British Government exploring, mapping and conducting politics in the Arab world. This text is an extract from a letter she wrote to her mother in 1893, when going to Persia by boat to meet her uncle, an ambassador.

- What do you think Bell thinks are good reasons for travelling?
- How does Bell seem to think people should behave overseas?

Letter Home

There are on board two English people of the most pronounced English type. He has travelled half the world over and is the most perfect specimen of globe trotter I have ever come across. I like the good stupid man: he enjoys what he can understand but then he can understand so very little. Petersburg [Sankt-Peterburg (St Petersburg, Leningrad)] is to him the place where they serve you three sorts of game for dinner, India the country of iced champagne; his one idea is to be able to say of a town or a sea or a continent "I have been there" no matter whether he has seen nothing of it. As for the wife, why she comes abroad I can't imagine for she has the meanest opinion of foreigners and their ways and their cooking. She dismisses the whole French cuisine at one blow:- they give you no potatoes "Now at home we always have potatoes and at least 3 vegetables with our meat!" She does her best to live exactly as if she were at home, but with ill success since everything is so unfortunately organised; she sat through the 6 o'clock dinner yesterday with an air of indignant protest and insisted on having coffee and bread and butter at the 2nd dejeuner to the great discomfiture of the waiters. I wonder she does not stay in England where she would have her accustomed shell all round her without any trouble.

TEXT 11

This text comes from *The Adventure of English* by Melvyn Bragg, a book that describes the history of the English language and how it has been influenced by historical events. The extract is taken from a chapter on the 17th century – a time of much exploration and travel.

- How many of these words had you realised were of foreign origin? Could you have guessed where they came from?
- English still 'borrows' words from other languages. Can you think of more words we use which originally came from other languages?

The Adventure of English

When English sailors encountered new foods and fruits and barrelled them up to try their luck in riverside markets of England, they brought the name or an Anglicisation of the original names with them: 'apricots' and 'anchovies', again from or via Spain and Portugal. 'Chocolate' and 'tomato' from French: though, a good example of the melting pot of language, 'tomato' could also be from the Spanish.

About fifty other languages joined the cargo of new words brought back in this period and swiftly integrated into English. In some cases there was an intermediary language. The language of the Renaissance bristled with imported words. 'Bamboo' (Malay); 'bazaar' (via Italian) and 'caravan' (via French) both Persian; 'coffee' and 'kiosk' (Turkish via French); 'curry' (Tamil); 'flannel' (Welsh); guru (Hindi); later there would be 'harem' and 'sheikh' and 'alcohol' (Arabic); 'shekel' (Hebrew); 'trousers' (Irish Gaelic). Off they went, English ships all over the world, trading in goods, looting language.

But this game or addiction was not confined to men on ships. It was a time when English artists, scholars and aristocrats began to explore Europe. Their preferred destination was Italy, the dominating culture of the time. There they were awestruck by the architecture, the art, the music, and brought back words which described what they saw and once again provided a platform for new ideas, in this case ideas about a cultural explosion, which England so far had heard mostly from an islanded distance.